WE HAVE WITH US TONIGHT

WITH US TONIGHT

By

E. A. CORBETT, LL.D.

Author of *Henry Marshall Tory,*
Father, God Bless Him, etc.

Introduction by

LEONARD BROCKINGTON, C.M.G., LL.D.

THE RYERSON PRESS ~ TORONTO

Published October, 1957

To Anna Rae

Foreword

THIS is not a reference book, nor is it primarily a history of adult education in Canada. It is an attempt to tell in an episodic and highly personal way some of my own experiences as a worker in this particular field. The people who appear in the following pages are given their real names, and the events recorded are as close to reality as my records and my memory can make them.

If it is true that the history of a country and its people can be illuminated by casual events and casual conversation, this book may have some value.

E. A. C.

Introduction

by

Leonard W. Brockington

IN THIS BOOK are set out some of the memories of a son of Canada, who knows his native land as few other men know her, and through a long life has served her highest causes with unselfish devotion in peace and in war. Many countries are happily blessed with dedicated sons and daughters, who deserve fame, but do not seek it, and only rarely attain it. They are men and women, who unmindful of material success, are content to keep their bank accounts and their securities in the hearts of their friends. Such a man is the author of *We Have with Us Tonight*. As one who has known the immeasurable joy of his friendship for over thirty-five years, I am happy to write a few words of introduction to this wise and exhilarating book.

Dr. Corbett was born in Nova Scotia, was educated at Huntingdon Academy in Quebec, received his B.A., and M.A., at McGill University, is a graduate of the Presbyterian Theological College, and an honorary graduate of Mount Allison University. He served in

England and France in the First Great War with
the ultimate rank of Acting Captain. He spent some
years thereafter in a Sanitarium for the Tubercular.
He has known much hardship, much suffering, and
deep personal sorrow. These things are not set down
in this book. For the ideals, which inspire his life and
will continue to inspire his fellow citizens, gave him
the strength which enabled him to rise above all his
misfortunes. In early manhood he settled in the
Canadian West. He was born in a Presbyterian
manse, and, like many such sons, he went into the
world with a sacrificial passion for education. He is
as Canadian as a dappled Maple tree, and long ago
was uplifted by a vision of Canada and a faith and a
hope in its civilization and the power of its own sons
and daughters to paint its pictures, to sing its songs,
and to record the annals of its history and social
progress. For in things which touch Canadian life
and its artistic expression, he has shared with many
others the creed that "the consciousness that an art
has grown up to maturity, from the very ground you
are treading, and is bearing its blossom and its fruit
all around you, is something different from the feeling
that it has been brought to you from a very long way."

During the last few decades we have all witnessed
the growth of educational movements in Canada, the
work of the Extension Departments of many Universities, the notable advance in adult education, the
contribution made by the Canadian Broadcasting
Corporation and by the National Film Board to the

unity, the understanding, the entertainment, and the education of our nation, the surging interest in the drama and the festivals of the drama, the fruitful studies and historic report of the Massey Commission, the growing and merited renown of the Banff School of Fine Arts, and the establishment of The Canada Council. It is in the nature of things that great movements outlive the parent spark and it would be typical of Dr. Corbett himself to claim no more than a small and humble part in these great happenings. But I know of no citizen of this country to whom their far beginnings owe so much as they do to the modest author of these memoirs for his unquenched enthusiasm and his unremitting labour.

According to the books of reference, he has been Director of the Extension Department of the University of Alberta, Director of the Canadian Association for Adult Education, President of The Canada Foundation, Governor of the Dominion Drama Festival, Director and Founder of the Banff School of Fine Arts, President of the Canadian Handicrafts Guild, President, Board of Directors, Alberta Drama League, and President of the Philosophical Society, University of Alberta. He is the author of four other memorable books, *McQueen of Edmonton,* a biography of Edmonton's great Presbyterian minister and missionary, *Blackfoot Trails,* a study of the Indians of Alberta, *Henry Marshall Tory, Beloved Canadian,* a tribute to the life and work of the First President of the University of Alberta, who was also President of the

National Research Council, and in the undying and still youthful enthusiasm of his old age, was the founder of Carleton College. Our author's other book, *Father, God Bless Him,* is a moving and wistful tribute to his own father, in whose devoted life can be seen so many of the shining virtues of his son. It deserves to survive as a little Canadian classic.

Of the man himself it is difficult to write without the superlatives of grateful friendship. Someone once said of Robert Louis Stevenson that whenever he entered a room it was as though another candle had been lit. It is the same with Edward Annand Corbett. He is a wonderful raconteur and the best mimic whom I know. For he has an uncanny capacity for capturing accents and mannerisms and for summing up in a flash a situation and a character. He has a poet's eyes, but though they may not roll in a fine frenzy, they gleam with fun. He possesses everything that is included in that indefinable phrase—a sense of humour. For with him it means a sense of proportion, a smiling derision of pomposity, what the author of *The Beloved Vagabond* once called, "turning the tears of life into a rainbow," and that enchanting gift which enables a man to take the iron out of his soul and transmute it into a gentle irony. He has always wanted to give to life a lift of merriment and to see us awaken to happy laughter over ourselves. In this book all these things are found in abundance.

Dr. Corbett lived in the West, (which is the fount and origin of many of these reminiscences), in the days when some of the old pioneers were still living and the magnificent eccentrics flourished, as it is hoped they will always flourish, on the frontiers of this land. In this book, therefore, are to be found sage and sagebrush philosophy and the history of worthwhile movements, which make it in a very real sense a great Canadian documentary lightened with glimpses of a lovable personality and brightened with the gold of a rare treasury of broad and deep humanity. Here also are a richness of stories and character sketches and hundreds of human touches which will make the pages sparkle in the eyes of the reader as the personality of the author sparkles in the company of his friends.

During the last few decades I have met Dr. Corbett in many places, for no one knows Canada any better than he does. I have seen him in the Far North, in the East, and in the West, and, in fact, in every part of our land. I remember his visits to England during the War and the work which he did for education amongst the troops. Two years ago, I met him unexpectedly in Jamaica, where he had been asked to do some work for UNESCO in the guidance of the awakening national consciousness of the West Indies along the pathways of progress and education. I expect any day to hear of him commuting between Ghana and Malaya helping new nations, as he has helped his own nation, along the highways and byways of democratic and artistic self-expression. Wherever I have met him, he has always been bubbling with enthusiasm, thereby exemplifying in his own vivid and irresistible personality the original meaning of enthusiasm, "The God Within." For he is certainly a man of daemonic and dynamic energy. He deserves our gratitude; for his life and work have enriched the land he loves and remain and will remain an abiding and beneficent influence to those who come after him.

Some years ago, Dr. Corbett retired from the Directorship of the Canadian Association for Adult Education. On the occasion of his retirement, a Banquet was held in his honour at the Arts and Letters Club in Toronto, and many tributes were paid to him. One came from Mr. George V. Ferguson, Editor of *The Montreal Star,* who is cherished amongst Dr. Corbett's oldest friends. It is written with such vitality, charm, truth and insight, that I have asked permission from the Publisher of this volume and the author of the tribute to include it in this Foreword. Mr. Ferguson's message of friendship is in itself as fine a piece of Canadiana as the reminiscences which are herewith launched on what it is hoped will be a happy voyage. These are the words of Mr. Ferguson written in honour of his friend and my friend, Ned Corbett:

This might be called a toast from absent friends. I am only one of them. But multiply me by "ten thousand times ten thousand in sparkling raiment clad" (to quote one of his favourite hymns) and you, who are present in the Arts and Letters Club tonight, will have some faint idea of the mighty cloud of witnesses to this evening's proceedings.

We are—we absent ones—a mighty queer lot, ranging from the drunken medical student beside whom your guest of honour lay in hospital in Edmonton in the winter of 1920 to the ghost of the late Willie Birks.

We include a thieving army batman and sundry sedate gentlemen in Geneva bands who admit that the inspiration of their ministry owes not a little to what they learned from a man named Corbett, who is as much at home riding in the Calgary Stampede as he is in the board room of the Royal Bank of Canada.

We include the Presbyterians among whom he was raised, the Catholics with whom he has laboured and swapped stories in Antigonish, and the academic and agnostic companions of his fishing and hunting trips in Alberta and British Columbia. Some of his best friends are Jews, and some are from Ontario.

And what do we unite in saying? Perhaps the most interesting thing about us is that we unite in nothing at all, save one thing only: our friendship, admiration and affection for your guest. He has helped us time and again. He has listened patiently to our stories and told us better ones of his own without rancour.

He has gossiped scandalously about us one minute, and the next has fearlessly mounted some barricade to protect our lives, our fortunes and our sacred honour, for, as one of us remarked to another some time back, he lacks courage not at all.

He has friends to the right of him, which makes enemies say he moves only with the big battalions. He has friends to the left of him, which makes others call him a bemused fellow-traveller. He has friends in front of him who, we hope, will volley and thunder in due course. But, so far as we are concerned, he has endless friends behind him, the oldest of which he picked up in a friendly way in his cradle, and the most recent became so as he came down town tonight.

Some of these friends call him "Doctor" respectfully. Others hail him casually as "You old rat." The difference lies only in the catholicity of his tastes. All alike have been touched by his mantle as he passed, a rich, warm coat of many colours which has more of Canada in its hemline than most men have in all their wardrobe.

He came by this the hard way but always with affection and a good measure of sentiment for, if the truth be told, your guest of honour is no tough guy. He is far too sensitive and perceptive for such a bluff.

It is inevitable that many members of your invisible guests this evening should be ghosts, for no man reaches past sixty with all the friends of his youth and middle years still spared to him. That accounts for those little petals of asphodel you may have noticed drifting down on you tonight. But a good many of us are left to join, even if remotely, in this biggest joke of 1951, the retirement of Edward Corbett.

Retirement! What a farce! He'll never retire. If he does, it will be because somebody has told him that old Charon, the ferryman, wants to hear the story about that Cape Breton molasses with "the queer, wild taste to it," and he'll cross the Styx to tell it to him.

Toronto, Ontario.

Contents

PART ONE

PART TWO

CONTENTS

PART ONE

1

My Debut as a Craftsman

NOVEMBER 10, 1917, was a big night at the Khaki College in Seaford, Sussex. The late Major R. W. Brock and I were in charge of the institution, and out of a possible 30,000 Canadian soldiers in the area we had a total enrollment of 2,000 officers and other ranks. They were studying everything from conversational French (*Voulez-vous promener avec moi ce soir, mademoiselle?*) through the three R's to bookkeeping, livestock judging, typing, history, English, advanced mathematics, and Greek.

We had recently gone a step further and arranged a series of monthly lectures as a means of bringing the students together from their isolated classrooms and giving the college a sense of community and solidarity. The first lecture a month before had been a tragic failure. A prominent industrialist from Montreal was in London and we invited him down to give a talk about Canada. He accepted our invitation and announced that he would speak on "Power." We naturally expected he would talk about some aspect of Canada's natural resources. I went over to Brighton and had several thousand dodgers printed, and on the night of the opening lecture in the series the big auditorium of the Central YMCA hut was packed to the doors. Unfortunately our guest speaker was a man of strong evangelical temper, and instead of talking about Canada's industrial potential he preached one of the dullest sermons I have ever listened to on moral and spiritual power. As soon as the trend of his remarks became apparent, slowly the men began to drift out of the place, and at the end of an hour the only people left in the audience were the Brigadier and his staff, who occupied the front seats, plus a few padres.

Now, for the second lecture, we were to have "Professor" A. E. Ottewell from the University of Alberta. I met him at the station. He was dressed in the uniform of a first lieutenant. I think he was the biggest man I had ever seen in uniform. His Sam Brown belt would have made a surcingle for a good sized bronco. He announced that he would give an illustrated lecture on "Evolution" and I was terrified at the thought of what might happen to him. Once again the auditorium was filled to overflowing, but this time no one left the hall until the last word had been spoken. First he got the men singing such old familiar favourites as "The Old Grey Mare," "I'm a

Little Prairie Flower," "Old Macdonald Had a Farm." Then, with earthy wit and spontaneous bellowing laughter at his own sallies, he held his audience spellbound for an hour. After that in England, and after the Armistice in France, the Canadian Army could never have too much of Ottewell.

I couldn't know then that this was the man I was to work with later in Alberta for many years, and who gave me whatever I have in the way of a working philosophy of adult education.

I spent two years in military hospitals after being invalided out of France in September, 1918; and here again I saw men wounded in mind and body fit themselves for normal return to civilian life through hard study and by taking advantage of the vocational training classes provided for the up-patients and the bed-patients as well. My lifelong interest in handicrafts began in Third London General Hospital, London, England, when a "ward aid" persuaded me to learn to knit. This was a tiny spinster of advanced years who was driven to the hospital every morning by a chauffeur in a huge Rolls-Royce. We knew her simply as "Sister," but an officer next to me who was an inveterate joker told me he had it on good authority that she was "Lady Diane Sharp-Cutt-Sharp, of Scisserton Manor, Knots." At any rate she was an expert in basketry, needlework, and knitting and she soon had most of the chaps in our Ward—about fifty altogether—at work. I chose knitting and I immediately embarked upon the creation of a woollen scarf. The

thing grew until it was four feet long, but it had
neither form nor comeliness. It started out to be eight
inches wide but it narrowed down to three in some
places and burgeoned out to ten in others. When
finished it looked like a cobra coiled and ready to
spring.

Six months later, when I arrived at the Balfour
Sanatorium on the Kootenay Lakes, B.C., I had an
opportunity to experiment in wider fields. There
were, in addition to the usual "ward aids" who taught
basketry and knitting, a well-equipped library, a
cabinetmaking workshop with a highly qualified
instructor in woodwork, and courses in shorthand and
typing. Here I embarked on a career as a craftsman
which later led me to great heights. In 1938 I was
elected (in my absence) President of the Canadian
Handicrafts Guild.

Fully aware by this time of the therapeutic values
in handicrafts, I became a basket-maker. This would
have been all to the good if I had kept to my first
passion, i.e. making sewing baskets. But the creative
instinct took possession of me, egged on by my
roommate, Captain Ned Sheppard, only son of E. E.
Sheppard, founder of Toronto *Saturday Night*. I had
been introduced to Ned Sheppard on the night of my
arrival at the San. He occupied a big double room
facing the lake, complete with private bath, etc. When
the matron took me up to his room and knocked on
the door, a voice from inside shouted, "Friend or
Enema?" Ned was lying on his bed in the semi-

darkness, and after the matron left he said: "They told me in France that I had a hole in my left lung as big as a beer-mug. I've been trying to keep it filled ever since. How about a smash right now?" Whereupon he lifted his emaciated six-foot-two frame, staggered to a dresser and produced a bottle of Johnny Walker from beneath a pile of pyjamas.

This was my brilliant and fascinating roommate for nearly a year. He was a dying man, plagued by frequent hemorrhages, but his cheerfulness and courage made our room a rendezvous for doctors, nurses, and a number of up-patients at all hours. He occupied himself with the publication of a weekly newspaper called *The Balfour Bugle,* which he typed out himself and had published in the city of Nelson. It contained each week one brilliantly written major article, news notes and ribald rhymes and jokes. The 175 patients waited eagerly each week for its appearance. Ned used to sing a song of his own composition every time a doctor entered the room. "Oh some have bronchitis and some have T.B., but it's only just dandruff that's a-botherin' me."

We were weighed every Monday, and if a man on exercise lost a pound or two during the week he was sent back to bed until he had recovered his losses. The Monday morning line-up was attended by one of the doctors and a nurse. The doctor weighed each patient in turn and the nurse entered up the poundage in her chart. It was an anxious time for everyone; an up-patient dreaded going back to bed and bed-patients were always hoping to gain enough to be allowed up. All sorts of tricks were played on the officials. Ned Sheppard, who had never been allowed on exercise but always hoped that he would eventually make it, stepped on the scales one Monday morning with a fire extinguisher hidden under his dressing gown. He still lost weight.

With Ned's encouragement I embarked upon two major feats of craftsmanship. I decided to make a wicker piano lamp. This was woven of heavy rattan, and after the broad base was finished the column, about eight inches in circumference, rose steadily upward. But in spite of all I could do the column began to lean outward from the base, and by the time it had reached its full height of seven feet, complete with woven shade, it looked like the leaning tower of Pisa. It had a brooding, threatening look, and years later, when it stood in a corner of the cellar in our home in Edmonton, the kids called it Boris Karloff.

My other major undertaking began after I became an up-patient and was allowed to spend a couple of hours a day in the woodworking establishment. There, under the watchful eye of the instructor, Mattie Matheson, I proceeded to build a mahogany library table. This took nearly a year to complete and became such a noted example of the craftsman's art that when at last, a few weeks before I left, the job was done, the whole staff of the Sanatorium turned out to celebrate the occasion. I was led out to the workshop by a Highland piper, playing The Road to the Isles. There, drawn up in a semicircle were about fifty people. I was led to the centre of the ring and told to kneel on a gilded cushion in front of one of the doctors, who was dressed like a medieval high priest. I was dubbed "Knight of the Gimlet and the Jack-plane," presented with a leather medal about half the size of a blacksmith's apron, and a citation praising my contribution to art. The table was carried out of the workshop to a horse-drawn cart bedecked with ribbons, and led by the piper the procession moved off to the cottage where my wife and two small boys lived. There a formal presentation was made and the table became a family possession. Sad to relate, it later took its place in the basement of our Edmonton home, close beside Boris Karloff; for, although it looked quite attractive, the truth is that nothing could ever make it sit even on the floor. Any attempt to use it as a writing table drove it into a frenzy of agitation.

It was shortly after this that I received a letter from Dr. H. M. Tory, President of the University of Alberta, offering me a job as assistant to A. E. Ottewell, Director of the Department of Extension, and in the fall of 1920 I left the Sanatorium and settled down in Edmonton to embark upon a career (if it can be called that) which has occupied me ever since.

2

Flashback

THIS was not my first experience in Alberta. I had spent seven months in the country as far back as 1904. I was attending Huntingdon Academy (Huntingdon, Quebec) and was in my second year there when, early in March, three months before the end of the term, I ran out of money. I had financed my first two years, through grades 9 and 10, by working during the summer as an assistant in the butter factory at Rockburn, Quebec (where my father was minister). I lived at home and my job was to appear at the plant about 4:30 a.m., get up steam in the boilers and be ready to weigh in the milk when the first farmers with their wagon loads began to appear—usually between 5.30 and 6 a.m. I was through my work for the day by twelve o'clock, then I hurried home, got a quick lunch and spent my afternoons haying, hoeing corn, picking apples, etc., depending upon the season. I was paid

$30.00 per month by the butter factory and I received 50c for an afternoon's work with a local farmer.

In that way I earned enough to pay my fees, buy books and clothing and have enough left over to pay for board and lodging throughout the school year. If I remember rightly, room and board cost about $2.50 a week.

But in my third summer I decided upon a change of occupation. I took out an agency for the sale of stereoscopic views. For the sum of $15.00 I got possession for the summer months of a small "drop-hipped" horse, borrowed a buggy from my father, and started off as a salesman. In those days no front parlour was complete without a collection of stereoscopic views, usually highly coloured photographs of the Holy Land, scenes from Scotland, etc., a few comic serials, such as "Pat Murphy's Honeymoon" or similar adventures. These were viewed through a stereoscope; a highly decorative piece of furniture fitting over the bridge of the nose and the forehead, with two enclosed windows of magnifying glass which somehow fused the double picture into an enlarged and surprisingly clear three-dimensional reproduction of the scene. Some of the wealthier farmers would have an album with as many as one hundred views, and visitors were often entertained for a whole evening looking at the sequences of a journey through Palestine or some other part of the world. The views sold for 25c, the salesman's commission was 15c, and of course the big deal was to start a family off on the road to higher education with a stereoscope—price $3.00, commission $1.50—and a couple of dozen pictures. But for the most part people already had the equipment and would perhaps buy a half-dozen new views, often because it was the minister's son and they were kind enough to give him a helping hand.

It was not a successful summer financially, although I met a lot of people and had a lot of fun, especially when I tried to sell my wares to a French-Canadian family. (*"Voulez-vous permettez-moi de vous montrer quelque choses"*—my French was terrible!)

Hence the situation in which I found myself in March, 1905. I had no money to pay for board and lodging until June, when I would finish the tenth grade. I am sure my father from his salary of $800.00 a year would have found some way to finance me through the term, but there were five more in the family, younger than I, to be educated, and I didn't want to add to the burden. One evening towards the end of March, I met downtown in Huntingdon a chap by the name of Bob Beatt. His father, Reverend James Beatt, had preceded my father as minister of the Rockburn congregation. Bob had gone west some years before this and now had a position as a porter at the Banff Springs Hotel at Banff, Alberta, during the summer months. He told me he could get me a job as a tourist guide at the hotel for the following summer if I wished. At that time the CPR operated its own tourist service at Banff and Lake Louise. The Brewster family, who later took over the agency, kept a livery stable on the main street of the town and I think owned the King Edward Hotel as well. Without consulting my family, I went in to Montreal a few days later and presented myself with Bob Beatt at the CPR employment office. After having given verbal proof of my horsemanship, I was duly signed on as guide, counsellor and friend to tourists at $40.00 per month "and found." I then returned home, and a week later, in company with six other men, left the Windsor station, Montreal, for the "wild and woolly west." We had been given tourist-car accommodation, but no provision was made for meals enroute; consequently we had provided ourselves with emergency rations in the shape of bread, canned salmon, crackers, etc., and depended on quick meals at the railway restaurants for the rest. It was a pleasant and for me an exciting journey; nevertheless I was glad when, three days later, early on the morning of April 12th (my birthday) we got off the train at the little town of Cochrane about thirty miles west of Calgary.

We were met at the station by a ranch-hand driving a three-seated buckboard, and after a chilly drive of twelve miles arrived at a long, low ranch-house in the foothills near the Ghost River. The boss man here was a fierce little fellow called Shorty McKay, but after a few days one discovered that the real boss, so far as the ranch-house itself was concerned, was the Chinese cook, to whom the men referred as One Lung. Only three of us had got off the train at Cochrane; the three other men in company with Bob Beatt had gone on to

Banff to help with the job of getting the hotel and grounds ready for the summer.

Our job was to herd a motley collection of cayuses, broncos, and half a dozen large cart horses through the foothill trails to Banff, where most of them were to be broken for riding and driving. The cart horses had been at work around the hotel the previous summer, but the cayuses and broncs for the most part were as wild and wary as coyotes. It took us the better part of three days to get that mixed bag of animals along the trails to Banff. The first night out we spent near the Stoney Indian Reserve at Morley. This was the easiest part of the trip; from here on it was tougher going. It was bitterly cold at night but, although there was still plenty of snow on the mountains, travelling along the winding trail by day in the bright spring sunlight was pleasant enough.

Our guide, and boss, was a lanky cowhand from the Cochrane ranch by the name of Oklahoma Pete, and at night around the campfire he entertained us with wildly exaggerated tales of his experience as a cowboy in the Western States and in Canada. During the day he occasionally broke into song. His favourite, The Cowboy's Lament, is a song well known to every rangeman, but he also included in his repertoire The Red River Valley, On Top of Old Smokey, and a song I was later to become acquainted with: It's the Rich wot Gits the Pleasure, It's the Poor wot Gits the Blime. Oky, as we called him, was also one of the most gifted liars I have ever met. It was from this character I first heard the story (which every Westerner has heard) of the amazing effects of the hot Chinook wind. Frequently in the winter months in Alberta the temperature will rise in a matter of minutes from below zero to 60 or 65 degrees above. Oky used to tell of an occasion when he was driving a team of horses hitched to bobsleds from Cochrane to Calgary. According to his story, he was driving the fastest pair of broncos in North America when halfway to Calgary he heard behind him the soft whisper of the Chinook wind. He immediately put the whip to his horses and for the next ten miles he made the trip with the runners of the rear sled on dry land and the front runners in deep snow.

On the afternoon of the third day we drove our horses up the Main Street of Banff to a big corral on the Bow river, about a half mile from the Banff Springs Hotel. For the next five weeks we spent our time getting the horses saddle-broken and ready for driving in pairs attached to two and three-seated buckboards. We lived in a long, low bunkhouse near the corral and had our meals in a cookhouse nearby. After the hotel opened in the latter part of May we were out every day either riding or driving along the trail to Devil's Lake, around Tunnel Mountain, and sometimes on week-long trips with fishing parties on the mountain trails leading to Emerald Lake and Lake Louise.

It was a happy, healthy and carefree life and I enjoyed every minute of it. We had been promised return fare to Montreal at the end of the season, which I think was the middle of September, but during the last week in August I was fired from the job and told to find my way back to Montreal or anywhere else for that matter—on my own. It happened this way. I had been out for three days with a party of three Germans —noblemen, Counts Von this and that. I spoke no German and they knew very little English, so there was almost no conversation. We had ridden out to Devil's Lake, where they put up at the CPR Chalet while I looked after the horses and lived in a bunk-house nearby. The fishing was excellent and we returned to Banff on Sunday well pleased with the expedition. I had at this time, as my pride and joy, a sorrel gelding who was by long odds the best saddle horse in the stable. He was rangy, fast and had enormous stamina, but he also had the most evil temper I have ever encountered in a horse. I had to keep him in a box-stall with his head tied near the door, and it was suicide to walk behind him until one of his front legs was strapped up and he was standing on three. Even at that he was dangerous. I kept a muzzle over his nose to keep him from biting my head off, and I really believe he could have stood on one leg and kicked with all the other three. I had him because no one else in our crew would be bothered with him.

On this occasion I came down from the hotel to our stables, riding my sorrel and leading the three broncos the Germans had used. I turned the broncos into the corral and put my horse in his box-stall, and went into the cookhouse for supper. When I came out, the stable boss, a giant of a man by the name of Trotter, was waiting for me.

"I see you've got a saddle gall on that sorrel gelding."

"I've never had a saddle gall on a horse in my life —there isn't a mark on him."

Trotter opened the door of the box-stall and started to walk around behind the horse, because the bare patch he took for a saddle gall was on the other side from the door. The gelding lit out with both hind feet and knocked Trotter sprawling. He was too close to the animal to be badly hurt, but he was humiliated and very angry. All might have been well if I hadn't burst out laughing. This infuriated him and he came at me shouting, "I'll teach you to laugh, you Quebec son of a bitch." I think if he had just called me a son of a bitch and let it go at that it wouldn't have been so bad, but making me out to be a particular kind of an s.o.b.—a Quebec one—somehow made me furious. He struck me a walloping blow in the pit of the stomach which doubled me over. Then he almost knocked me cold with a left hook to the chin.

I had a half-gallon oat dipper in my right hand, and as Trotter came at me again I brought the dipper down on the top of his head with all the strength I had left. It was more than enough. He flopped on the stable floor and I ran to the bunkhouse. I was pretty sure he would kill me unless I had a friend or two to back me up. In a few seconds he came roaring into the bunkhouse, but there were four of us now and more than he cared to tackle. He stood glaring at me for a minute and then shouted "Get the hell out of here and don't come back."

Thus for the first and last time in my life I was fired from my job. The hotel bookkeeper paid me off, but refused to give me transportation back to Montreal. I packed my belongings, went downtown and got a room at $1.00 a night in the Park Hotel (long since gone from Banff's Main Street). Some time before this Rev. Alex. Gordon (son of Dr. Gordon, Principal of Queen's), who was Minister of the Banff Presbyterian Church at the time, had left a note at the bunkhouse to say that he had had a letter from my father asking him to look me up. The note invited me to call on him whenever I could find time. But we were kept on the go every day, including Sunday, from dawn till dark and I had never had a chance to accept his invitation. The morning after I was fired, I decided to look him up. He lived in a two-room shack just behind Brewsters' Livery stable. He had three preaching appointments: Canmore, Banff, and a mining camp (now closed) between Banff and Devil's Lake.

When I called he was preparing his midday meal and he invited me to share it with him. During the meal I told him of my adventure of the day before. I could see that he was secretly amused by my treatment of the stable boss, but did not wish to appear enthusiastic about violence of any kind. He asked me what I intended to do. I explained that I had saved over $150.00 out of my pay and tips, but that I would have to pay over $50.00 for a second class ticket to Montreal and the balance would not be sufficient to finance my final year at Huntingdon Academy. He urged me not to give up my dream of a university education even if I had to miss a year through lack of money.

That afternoon I wandered about Banff not quite decided whether to look for another job or return to Huntingdon at once in time to start the fall term the first week in September. I was offered a job as bus driver and part time bartender for the Park Hotel at $45.00 a month and board, but when I mentioned this proposal that night at supper Alex Gordon said, "Don't touch it; give us a day or two and we can do better than that. Meanwhile give up that room at the hotel and move in here with me." He had an extra bed and I was glad to accept his invitation.

The next day I met Joe Brown, head porter at the Banff Springs Hotel. Joe said, "Bob Beatt told me about your row with Trotter. I've known that guy for a good many years and I was glad to hear you socked him; he's had it coming for a long time. What are you going to do now?" I told Joe I wanted to get back to finish my schooling, but couldn't afford the passage to Montreal. Joe thought about that for a while, then he said, "Come on down to the station tomorrow morning at ten o'clock when the Imperial Limited from Vancouver goes through, maybe I can get you on board." The next day I took my small

trunk and suitcase down to the station and while
Bob Beatt, who was second porter, looked after the
passengers who were going up to the hotel, Joe rushed
me back to the dining-car and spoke to the dining-car
conductor and told him about my predicament. The
dining-car conductor said, "I could use an extra
hand in the kitchen, washing dishes, peeling potatoes,
making ice-cream and so on. I can't pay anything, but
if the lad wants to take a chance it's all right with me."
Joe checked my trunk through to Montreal (don't ask
me how he did it) and a few minutes later when the
train pulled out of the Banff Station I was in a white
coat washing breakfast dishes in one of the two
dining-cars.

It was a hot and steamy job, and that night when
we finally bedded down in the dining-car I comforted
myself with the thought that it was only three more
days to Montreal and the ordeal would be over. But
an unkind fate ruled otherwise. At some divisional
point between Regina and Winnipeg, and while I was
sound asleep, our car was "kicked off" the east-bound
train and attached to the west-bound. When I woke
up I was dismayed to find that I was on the way back
to where I came from. To make a long story as short
as possible, I was ten days on that dining-car before
we finally pulled into Windsor Station. We had gone
all the way back to Vancouver, and after a few days
lay-over in that city we started eastward again.

Every morning I was up at 5 a.m. helping the cooks
get ready for the first breakfasts. All day long I washed

dishes, peeled potatoes, turned the handle of an enormous ice-cream freezer and generally made myself useful around the kitchen. I was dirty, greasy and desperately weary when I finally arrived home, but it was worth it. I had enough money to complete my final year at Huntingdon Academy.

Thus ended my first experiences in Alberta.

I was destined to see much more of the Province of Alberta in the years to come. After matriculation I returned to the Cochrane ranch for a long and somewhat routine summer of range-riding, and while I was taking my degrees in Arts and Theology at McGill, I served three summers on Alberta Mission fields—from 1907 till 1910. The first of these experiences, at Beaver Lake, in 1907 I have described elsewhere.[1] In the spring of 1908 I was assigned by the Home Mission Board of the Presbyterian Church to a mission field in Northern Alberta, which covered a much wider area than I had had the previous summer. My home base here was at St. Eugene on the old Athabasca Trail about fifteen miles north of Fort Saskatchewan. There were four preaching appointments—at Succer Creek, Foam Lake, St. Eugene and Patricia. Two of them I took one Sunday and the other two the following week. The round distance was roughly 100 miles, and I spent my days in the saddle. That summer I covered more than 2,000 miles on horseback. I lived on the MacLean brothers' horse ranch. This was a household of three wealthy Scots

[1]*Father, God Bless Him;* The Ryerson Press, Toronto, 1953.

bachelors, and the establishment was served by a bachelor nephew who was cook, housekeeper, dairy· man, poultryman, and the only male in the area who drove a buggy into Fort Saskatchewan and wore an apron in the kitchen.

It was a great and glorious summer, that summer of 1908, for when I was not on the trail visiting my parishioners I was helping Hector MacLean break horses. That may be why the brothers would never allow me to pay a cent for board and room.

I mention these pioneer experiences here only to point up the fact that when I left the Sanatorium at Balfour in the fall of 1920 to become assistant to A. E. Ottewell in the Department of Extension at the University of Alberta, I had already seen a good deal of the Province in which I was to spend the next sixteen years.

3

Alberta Days and Nights

IT WOULD have been difficult to find a kinder or more considerate boss than Albert Ottewell. He insisted that for a year at least I should take it easy as assistant director of the Department of Extension. I was to look after administration while he was away, which was nearly ninety percent of the time; edit the monthly *Press Bulletin*; and make whatever decisions had to be made, during his absence. On no account was I to undertake lectures or night work of any sort until I had recovered from my long illness.

In 1912 the University of Alberta had graduated its first class of students. Ottewell was one of them. He had taken first-class honours in classics and philosophy, and although he could scarcely see two feet without his glasses he had had a crushing record as a football player. He had been brought up on a pioneer farm in Clover Bar, Alberta, in the tough closing years of the last century. He told me that sometimes his father used to waken his large family of boys in the morning by shouting up the ladder to the loft where they slept: "Roll out boys, daylight in the swamp; no rabbits, no breakfast!" Apparently there were times in those days when that was not by any means a novel situation.

When Ottewell graduated he was actually headed for the ministry and had already served as student preacher on Alberta mission fields. But Dr. H. M. Tory, the founder and president of the University, with his keen eye for men of quality, had another idea for young Ottewell's future. He had decided that a university which depended for its existence on the taxes of the people should be in a position to provide some sort of recognizable *quid pro quo*. In discussing the job of University Extension, Dr. Tory used to say:

This establishment, in addition to capital expenditure in building and equipment, costs the people of Alberta over half a million dollars a year. Many of them will never see the place, much less have an opportunity of attending or having their children attend its classes. Yet we want the citizens of the Province to feel that the University belongs to them, that it exists to serve them. The time may come when the existence of a university will depend on the public's assurance that its thinking and research are of vital importance to the community. The job of the Extension Department is to find out from the people what the University can do for them beyond the classroom and the laboratory.

It was thus that Dr. Tory chose Ottewell, in 1912, to be the director of the newly established Department of Extension. He couldn't have chosen a better man. With incredible energy and with great skill and understanding he built up one of the best-equipped organizations of its kind on the continent. When I joined the department in 1920 there were close to 300 travelling libraries in constant circulation throughout the Province; an open-shelf library of 15,000 volumes circulated by mail to people remote from ordinary library services; a package library system of materials for use by debating and discussion clubs; several hundred boxes of lantern slides used by schools and churches; and a moving picture library with, I think, about 100 films. Short courses were provided, lecture courses arranged, correspondence courses in economics sent out. Agricultural instruction in soils, marketing, livestock, etc., were all provided by a vigorous Provincial Department of Agriculture. Our job was to bring to the remote places of the Province whatever cultural and entertainment values the University could offer as a means of encouraging community solidarity, strengthening morale, awakening the civic conscience in regard to better home and school conditions; to bring colour and some kindliness into the hard and lonely lives of frontier people.

It was to this kind of life, with its wide variety of experience, that Ottewell introduced me.

During the sixteen years in which he served as director of the Department he travelled continuously over dreadful roads, and no roads at all, in a Model T. Ford coupe. The battered Ford car he drove was tilted by his weight from the driver's seat at a downward angle of about 40 degrees. From the rear it always seemed to be proceeding at terrific speed with a sideways, crab-like motion. To pull his car out of the everlasting mudholes of the Alberta roads, he had an ingenious device, by means of which he could fasten a rope to a distant tree or telephone pole, the other end wrapped around an enormous projecting rear-wheel hub. Thus he would force the groaning engine to do its own dirty work. I never could understand how that contraption managed to conquer a five-foot hole of gumbo, but it did.

He was over six foot tall and weighed, at the time I joined him, close to 300 pounds, mostly solid bone and muscle. I know this because one day we attended the Edmonton Exhibition together and as we wandered along the Midway we came upon a huckster with a set of spring scales. He was offering for the small price of 25c to guess the weight of any man in the crowd around him. If he missed by more than three pounds, his customer was awarded a box of chocolates. We watched this chap performing for a while and were, both of us, amazed at the accuracy with which he could gauge a man's weight. He would run his hands swiftly over his victim's body, then turn to the crowd and say, "Well I guess this baby weighs about 173½ pounds." As long as we watched him he was never more than a pound or two wrong. This intrigued

Ottewell, and he said to me, "I think I can fool him." He stepped up, gave the man a quarter and as usual the latter ran his hands over Ottewell's chest and thighs, then shouted, "Well I guess this little cutie pie will run about 250 pounds." Ottewell sat down on the spring seat and the indicator shot up to 298 and stayed there. The pitch man looked at his scales in complete amazement. Then he handed Ottewell a box of chocolates, grabbed him by the back of the neck, and to the vast amusement of the crowd shouted, "Get outta here; you're full of wet hay."

Ottewell's voice, his laughter, his appetite, his energy and stamina were Gargantuan. He was a kind of educational Paul Bunyan. He thought nothing of spending most of the night with a group of farm people, say at Pincher Creek in Southern Alberta, and then starting at daylight—after consuming a couple of cans of salmon, which was his favourite breakfast—to conduct a similar meeting the following night at Coronation, about 300 miles away. And this was in the days when there were few, if any, highways.

He was a man of outspoken opinions, and after the Farmer's Government was elected in Alberta in 1921 Ottewell, who was an ardent Liberal, was frequently in trouble because of his attacks upon what he called "Group Government." Once he arrived in a Northern Alberta Community to give a lecture (at the invitation of the local school board) and found no one to welcome him; but the school house was open, so he lit a fire, swept a week's filth out of the place, filled the woodbox and sat down to wait for his audience. Before he was through with his talk that evening he made the sweeping statement that if you wanted to find the most ignorant, inefficient man in the average Alberta community you had only to look for the chairman of the local school board. That remark in those years had just enough truth in it to hurt, and Ottewell almost lost his job over it. One of Ottewell's most popular lectures was his illustrated dissertation on Evolution. At some time or other almost every school district in Alberta had heard it. I have no doubt it was of great and lasting value, but it was a source of constant annoyance to Dr. Tory, who received regular protests from those communities in which The Calgary Bible Institute or some other fundamentalist group had found a foothold. Ottewell was known and welcomed in every community in Alberta, from the Peace River to the Montana border and from Lloydminster in the east to Rocky Mountain House in the west.

One of my first trips as an Extension lecturer was a month-long journey to the Peace River country. Arrangements had been made jointly by W. D. Albright, Director of the Dominion Experimental Farm at Beaver Lodge, and Major E. C. Clark, who was regional Director of the Department of Veterans' Affairs for the Peace River country. There were to be short courses for soldier farmers and their wives at Grande Prairie, Spirit River, Beaver Lodge and other settlements in the area. I was to leave Edmonton on

the Peace River train early in October, 1922. On all
such journeys I carried along a 28 mm. moving picture
machine, with a twelve-volt battery, and a large
collection of films; a slide projector, with several boxes
of slides; a box of books and pamphlets; and in
addition my own suitcase and a shotgun in case I
encountered an invasion of prairie chicken, mallards
or wild geese (a consummation devoutly to be
wished.)

One of my problems as an Extension lecturer was
my utter lack of mechanical adroitness. The slide
projector was a simple enough gadget, but getting the
thing set up, the light properly adjusted, making
sure that the battery was fully charged, were always
worrying details; besides I was always getting the
slides upside down, or sideways. The moving picture
machine was a horror to me; getting the film threaded
onto the sprockets, adjusting the lens, keeping the
crank in place were bad enough, but I had a chronic
habit of forgetting to watch the take-off reel. Dozens
of times I would be cranking away vigorously in a
darkened school room only to wake up and discover
that the take-off had long ceased to function and film
was slithering all over the floor, under the benches
and around the feet of the audience. I would have to
stop the show, pile the unwound film into a basket or
any receptacle I could find, then proceed with the
picture. The business of re-winding the film and
repairing the breaks used to keep me busy far into
the night.

A day or so before I was scheduled to start on my journey to the Peace River, a letter was received at the department asking that I be allowed to stop off for a couple of days at a new settlement about one hundred miles north of Edmonton. This was a community opened up for homesteading in 1919, and about fifty families of Old Country soldiers, mostly Scotsmen, had taken up homesteads together in the heavily wooded country. They needed help in a number of ways and had turned to the University for advice.

In those days the Peace River train left Edmonton about 11 p.m. and crawled slowly on its way through bush and over heavy muskeg swamps, to arrive at MacLennan late in the afternoon of the following day. Here that section of the train going to Peace River Crossing turned north and the Grande Prairie, Spirit River, Beaver Lodge section continued westward. About five o'clock in the morning I was deposited on a small siding made of railroad ties and there I waited in the cold, grey dawn of a late October morning until eight a.m. To keep myself from freezing I had started a fire, and during my three hours of waiting the only readily available supply of firewood was the railroad ties out of which the platform had been built. By the time I was picked up I had burned up one layer of the landing stage. Given an hour or so longer, I might have established some sort of a record: "Man burns down railroad station to keep self from freezing." Presently I heard the sound of a team of horses and a wagon approaching along a logging road which led from the railroad straight east into the bush. A moment later I saw a pair of dappled grey Percheron horses, attached to a farm wagon and driven by a husky man of about thirty-five years of age.

"The name's McGregor."

"Glad to meet you."

"Ye've got quite a bit of gear with ye."

"Yes, moving picture machine, films — stuff like that."

"Well, we'll just have to make a box for this go-cart."

There was no box of any sort on the wagon, only the stringer between the front wheels and the rear. Mac took an axe, which was attached by a leather holder to the wagon pole, and in a few minutes had chopped down and fitted into place enough young poplars to make a floor on which to load my luggage and equipment and in a few minutes we were on our way back over the logging road towards the settlement. The trail was so rough that we could proceed only at a snail's pace, around stumps and over hillocks. As we crawled along, Mac told me about the people in the district. "We've just been in here about two years and are only getting started. But last year we all got together and built a big log community centre. It is to serve as school house, church, dance hall and theatre. We have a young bachelor here by the name of Pike. He's a Cambridge man; got shot up in the war and was sent in here by the Soldier Settlement Board. He has a degree in agriculture from some college in England. He's a great guy and I don't know what we'd have done without him. Most of us know mighty little about farming and he's taught us a lot."

About an hour and a half later, we came to a small ten-acre clearing, with a log-house, barn and corral in the middle of it. It didn't look like much from the outside, but inside it was warm and cosy. There was a lean-to kitchen, a living-room and two small bedrooms off to one side. In the centre of the living-room was a big box stove. Somehow Mrs. MacGregor had managed to make her home in the wilderness look like a little corner of England. There were the bits of good furniture; the polished brass knick-knacks that English women somehow manage to take with them wherever they go. There were a few good pictures and all over the place photographs of her people and the old home in Surrey.

While we were having breakfast, Mrs. Mac, who had been looking across the table at me, suddenly remarked, "Weren't you in Third London General Hospital in the fall of 1918? You were in one of those little turn-around huts in the orchard, just outside Ward K. I was one of your nurses." Then I knew why this little dark woman had looked so familiar. The two of them had settled on their homestead in January, 1919, just when the flu' epidemic was at its worst. Mac had gone to work in a lumber camp twenty miles away. This was before their house had been built and Mrs. Mac spent the winter with a neighbour woman, whose husband was also in the bush. As soon as it became known that she was a trained nurse Mrs. Mac was in demand everywhere, and during the months of February and March, when the temperature was frequently thirty or forty below zero, this plucky little woman travelled with a horse and a sleigh all over the district, caring for the sick and the dying. One story she told me that day I shall never forget. It illustrates the indomitable courage of women on the frontier.

One morning early a little girl about ten years of age rode into the yard and, crying bitterly, begged Mrs. MacGregor to come and help her mother who was very ill. Mrs. Mac harnessed the horse at once and started to follow the child home. It was 28 below zero. After a drive of four miles, they came to the "Russell place." Andy Russell was working at the same lumber camp as Mac, and the wife was alone on the homestead with her two children. Mrs. Russell was in bed and as soon as Mrs. Mac examined her she knew the woman was dying. She had kept on working too long and now it was too late to do anything for her. That afternoon the woman died and there followed an episode so heroic that it needs to be told here, if only to illustrate the hardships and sacrifices of the women who followed their men into the frontier homesteads of the north country thirty-five years ago.

After Mrs. Russell died, Mrs. Mac bundled the two children up as warmly as possible and drove them over to the homestead where she herself was living. After leaving them there she returned to the Russell home. She wrapped the body in blankets, and dragged the dead woman out to the tiny log stable and made a bed for her in the hay. This was necessary because of the speed with which decomposition would take place in a heated house. Then she stoked up the stoves in the house with coal and started off on her lonely journey. Shortly after she started it began to snow heavily and she could only proceed at a snail's pace as the horse picked out the trail leading to the camp. Once she got off onto a road and was forced to spend an hour or more retracing her steps to the main road again. It was daylight the next morning when, half frozen, she reached the camp. It was heart-breaking news she had to tell, but as soon as she had had some food she insisted that they start the return journey. By this time the trail was drifted high with snow and it was late in the afternoon when they arrived back at the Russell home. All that night Mac and the bereaved husband heaped brush and logs on a huge fire back in the bush a few hundred yards from the house in order to thaw out the ground so that a grave could be dug. The next afternoon a tiny group of neighbours stood beside the lonely grave—the first in the district— while Mrs. Mac from her little Prayer Book read out the burial service.

4

Macbeth in Homespun

AFTER BREAKFAST the following day, Mac and I took the team and wandered along the trails, knocking over an occasional prairie chicken and dropping in on the neighbours. We had lunch at Jimmy Callendar's place, which was only a mile or so from the Community Hall.

That night at about 6.30 the hall began to fill up with men, women and children, who had driven in their heavy farm wagons distances of from five to ten miles to hear what I had to say, and to see the pictures. Outside in the moonlight, horses were unhitched, blanketted, and tied to the rear of the wagons which were filled with hay for their feed. I met then some of the finest people I have ever known.

There was Captain Mahood, his wife and two sons. He was an Irishman who had spent all his life in the British Navy, a most genial, lovable person who, with his double-breasted blue suit and wing collar, his clean-shaven, sharp-featured face, looked as though he had just stepped off the bridge of a cruiser. His homestead was about two miles from the hall. There was Roy Newnham, a bachelor, with his brother Pat and his wife. They were from the Isle of Wight. There was Dave High and family, brother-in-law of the Callendars where we had lunched. They were from the north of Scotland. There was Bill Garth and his four sons, from Lancashire; the Johnston brothers, twins from London; there was Bill Rennie, late pilot in the R.F.C. There was Mr. A. C. Cushing, who operated a sawmill at Jarvie, five miles away, and who had donated the lumber for the roof and floors of the hall; Mr. and Mrs. Leslie Trickett, from somewhere in the north of England. Mrs. Trickett, who was a kind of godmother to the whole community, was one of the greatest cooks I have ever known. All these people I was meeting for the first time were in the next sixteen years to become my close and cherished friends.

The hall had a good kitchen at the back and the dinner was served piping hot; chicken, turkey, potatoes, turnips, salads, pickles, pies of every sort—it was a joy to behold and to eat.

That night after the show I crawled wearily into Captain Mahood's double wagon, and we humped our way over a stump-lined trail to a log house in a little ten-acre clearing. The Captain's driving was more or less by dead reckoning, since it was pitch dark and the trail as twisted as the convolutions of a sea serpent.

Once the tail-board "came adrift," and once a neighbour was invited "to step over the starboard whiffletree and come aboard." But safely settled in the warm little home over tea and pipes the dangers and discomforts of the voyage were forgotten, and with the good skipper I sailed the seven seas, and visited many lands until at four bells we piped down for the night.

Subsequently I visited the skipper on many occasions, and together we drank enough tea to float one of the cruisers he commanded during the first war, and smoked enough tobacco to ration the crew for a fortnight. On one of these visits I heard from him the story of how the local dramatic society put on Macbeth in the same log school and community hall in which I have so often lectured.

"It was like this. We arrived here in the spring of 1919, and we lived in a tent until with the help of the neighbours we had managed to build a house and barn. I was fresh from the sea, and did not know stem from gudgeon on horse, plow or wagon.

"One day when I was doing my best to get a team of horses to plow a straight furrow, along the trail from town a lad came riding a buckskin pony. He wore no hat, and rode in the full glare of a burning sun as if he loved the sting of it on his cheeks and his bared chest.

"He tied up his horse and crossed the field toward me walking with a marked limp. Pike was his name, he said. Captain Pike, late of His Majesty's forces during the recent display of temper in France, but now of the Soldier Settlement Board. How was I getting on? But a man can't talk in a field. Tea and tobacco—that's the ticket—without them there is no conversation worthy of the name.

"Well, he turned out to be a great fellow, this man Pike. He was here two years, and everything worth-while in this district we owe to him. Under his direction we built a community hall, put on plays, began experimenting with pure seed, organized a United Farmers' Association and generally began to get together as a community. But his greatest achieve-ment was the production of Macbeth. He had every man, woman, child, dog and cat in the neighbourhood in on that. And believe me—as you Canadians say—it was *some* show. Costumes were made out of sacking dyed in various colours. Armor was made from sheets of tin painted with some sort of silver-coloured paint. In every household Shakespeare reigned supreme, and after the cast was selected there was much burning of the midnight oil in studying the parts. I visited one house where Lady Macbeth was washing dishes and murmuring to herself: 'What, will these hands ne'er be clean? All the perfumes of Arabia will not sweeten this little hand.' In another place a chap cleaning his hunting knife, whistles through his teeth: 'Out damned spot! out, I say!' And Pike was everywhere. He was to play Macbeth, and even in his sleep he muttered: 'Tis some poor player that struts and frets his hour upon the stage.' The three witches were from one household, and the father told me: 'Lord knows what goes into the pot these days with them girls dancing around the stove with their Double, double toil and trouble; fire burn and cauldron bubble.'

"Pike wrote the University suggesting that a critic be sent up from the Department of Extension of the University, and the late John Blue, at that time provincial librarian, consented to go. Little Jimmy McTavish met him at the train, and Mr. Blue declares that when he knocked at the door of the house where he was to stay someone inside shouted: 'Here's a knocking indeed; if a man were porter of hell-gate he should have old turning the key. Who's there in the name of Beelzebub?'

"Once when rehearsing at the home of a hitherto patient farmer, Macbeth, played by Pike, had just declared, 'Sleep no more. Macbeth does murder sleep,' when a voice from the next room was heard, 'I'll say he does; hurry up and git the son of a gun murdered, or I'll come out there and do it myself.'

"Well, it was a wonderful time! The night of the show the hall was packed to the doors; there were people there who had travelled sixteen miles in grain wagons to see the performance. The cast was so big that at one time or another pretty nearly everybody in the audience had to rush up to the stage. Behind the scenes there were all sorts of mechanical noise-makers, a little sort of churn full of dried peas for hail, a thunder and wind machine combined that Pike had invented, and piles of swords and armour for marching troops.

"John Blue sat back by the stove, and when he was not biting the end of a cigar he was swallowing a lighted cigarette. I watched him, and the look of amazement never left his face except once when the sleep-walking Lady Macbeth shifted her chewing gum to the other cheek. Most of the time he made notes, and was solemn as an owl. It was an amazing spectacle to see, and for the most part exceptionally well done. When Macbeth appeared armoured for battle and began:

> Hang out our banners, on the outward walls
> The cry is "Still they come, our castles'
> Strength will laugh a siege to scorn," etc.

the play had become a living thing, the various parts had pieced themselves together, and even the actors saw it for the first time as a whole. In the part of Macbeth, Pike was magnificent. He had a Robert Mantell voice and bearing, and as he intoned the well-known words 'tomorrow and tomorrow, and tomorrow creeps in this pretty pace from day to day,' there was a silence broken only by an occasional gasp as of some one struggling with an unfamiliar emotion.

"What had threatened at the beginning to be a farce, before the end became an impressive performance. An elevation of spirit, a stirring of the emotions took possession of audience and players until the final curtain brought us all back to reality again.

"After the show John Blue spoke in glowing words of his pleasure in the production; he touched lightly on its weaknesses, and stressed rather the cultural value of a community effort of this kind.

"Yes, we shall not soon forget Pike. He was a Cambridge man, idealist, dreamer and lover of men, good and wholesome through and through."

"Where is he now?" I asked.

"In the soldiers' plot in Edmonton, dear chap. War wounds and overwork. There's only a small headstone to mark his place there, but up here his monument is everywhere."

5

Visitors from England

IN FEBRUARY, 1926, the University of Alberta was host to a team of student debaters from the British Isles. The team was made up of Hugh Molson, President of the Oxford Union at the time; J. P. McDonald, from the University of Edinburgh; and a chap from the University of Birmingham by the name of Nunn May (I think this was the scientist who achieved international notoriety a few years ago when he was convicted of being a Russian collaborator in Great Britain). These lads had been mopping the floor with Canadian student debating teams at Mc-Gill, Queen's, Toronto, Manitoba and Saskatchewan Universities. They were brilliant, witty, completely relaxed, and in most instances they proved to be too skilful for the more serious, cumbersome style of the Canadians. The subject for the debate at the University of Alberta was "Resolved that Civilization is a

failure." The Alberta debating team was made up of
Clarence Campbell (who is now President of the
National Hockey League), Walter Herbert (now
Director of the Canada Foundation), and James M.
Manson (now public liaison officer for the National
Research Council in Ottawa). If my memory serves
me, the Alberta team suffered the same mauling as
most of the other Canadian debaters.

At any rate, the old country lads had a week off in
Edmonton before proceeding to the University of
British Columbia, and the day after their performance
at the University of Alberta, Dr. Tory asked me to
come to his office and see him. In his office were
Molson and McDonald, and after the usual introduction Dr. Tory said: "These young men feel they are
being cheated. They have been all the way across
Canada and have never been outside of the cities.
Before leaving they would like to see something of the
country and how people live on the frontier." This
was on a Monday, and that afternoon I put through a
long distance call to Roy Newnham at Jarvie and asked
him to arrange a meeting in the community hall for
the next night.

Early Tuesday morning, with D. E. Cameron, the
university librarian, accompanying me, we picked up
McDonald and Molson at the Macdonald Hotel (Nunn
May elected to proceed to Vancouver and therefore
did not make the trip) and started on our journey of
ninety miles. It was a raw, cold day and the roads were
in fearful condition. There had been a Chinook over

the weekend and following that the mud and wet snow had frozen into ruts so deep that it was possible to drive the car almost without touching the steering gear. When we met a car coming towards us in the same two ruts we had a difficult time to pass.

It happened at that time that the Department of Extension owned two Model T Fords, one for Ottewell and one for myself. Mine was an open job with flapping curtains. It had seen pretty rough usage and was not in too sound condition. Our plan was to have breakfast at St. Albert, an historic little village twenty miles north of Edmonton. Here a well-known character, Scotty McNeil, kept a tidy little hotel which was famous for good food. Scotty was born on the Ile d'Orleans, Quebec, of a Scottish father and French-Canadian mother. He spoke French, English and some Gaelic.

As we ploughed our way toward St. Albert, on three different occasions we had to get out and literally lift the car out of the way of traffic coming into Edmonton. Meanwhile I talked, as I thought, rather brightly, about the early history of the trail we travelled and the countryside around us. This was too much for Molson, who sat beside me in the front seat. "I say, old chap, hope you don't mind, but I'm afraid I rather deplore people who chatter before breakfast." After that, nothing was said by anyone until we reached St. Albert. I had telephoned Scotty the night before and he had a piping hot, enormous breakfast ready for us. After breakfast and before we resumed our journey,

Molson turned to Scotty. "Have you a reah heah?"
This was beyond Scotty's comprehension and he looked
at me and said, "What he's mean, dat fellow?" "Oh,
he means a backhouse." Scotty's face beamed with
pride as he waved his arms and shouted, "Oh, sure,
sure, sure! We've got three of dem."

It took us all day to make the trip. Once we lost a
rear tire, torn loose from its moorings by frozen ruts.
We were moving so slowly that Cameron opened the
rear door on his side of the car and looked back at the
trail. "Hey, wait a minute Corbett, I think we've run
over a man." I stopped the car and got out. The right
rear tire casing had long ago disappeared and the
blood-red inner tube, badly chewed up, was dragging
along behind us, firmly attached at one end to the axle.
It did look a bit like a battered human being. In those
days one didn't change a wheel, one clamped on
another tire. As I struggled to replace the lost tire,
McDonald, who was a medical student, said, "If you
will hand me the case of instruments, I can tighten up
the nuts on the other wheels." This was the first time
I had ever heard a greasy old gunny sack, with monkey
wrench, pliers, a jack, etc., referred to as "a case of
instruments."

Not far from the village of Jarvie, an ancient derelict
by the name of Morrison lived in a dugout on the
banks of the Pembina River. He made his living by
trapping, and selling "moonshine likker" which he
brewed on the premises. I decided that since the Old
Country boys wanted to see how people lived on the

frontier, they might as well meet old Angus Morrison. We parked the car by the side of the road and walked down the hill to the river bank. There was a cloud of steam pouring out of Morrison's dugout and when we knocked on the door, he welcomed us warmly. "Ye're just in time. I'm running off a fresh brew. Ye'll have a drink." Cameron and I were familiar with the horrible stuff and begged off, but Molson said, "I'm descended from a long line of brewers, thank you very much!" He and McDonald, with much gasping and choking, downed a cupful each of the scalding liquid and we proceeded on our way.

We arrived at Jarvie about seven o'clock, having been seven hours on the road. The hall was jammed with people and the first sitting of a chicken dinner had been served and the second was on its way.

After the dinner and the dishes had been cleared away, I ran off two or three reels of film and then Molson addressed the gathering. He was in a jovial mood and opened his remarks by saying, "I notice there are a lot of Scotsmen here tonight," and Captain Mahood, smoking his pipe in the front row, shouted in his soft Irish brogue, "Yes, indade, but gophers is our worst pest." This remark produced roars of laughter and created the easy, relaxed mood which put Molson at his best. He spoke for an hour, and every face glowed with happiness as he told them of life in the British Isles since the war. After that McDonald's turn came. He was wise enough to realize the time had come for a change of pace, and for the next half hour he had his audience roaring as he sang the songs and patter of Harry Lauder and finished up reciting Burns' "Cotter's Saturday Night."

That night we all bedded down in Roy Newnham's cozy log house. Captain Mahood and his two sons came in to say good-night, but the talk went on until the small hours.

During the next few days, Molson, McDonald, Cameron, Roy Newnham and I visited every home in the district. At the end of the week we drove back to Edmonton worn out. I drove my guests to the Mac-Donald Hotel, but we were so covered with mud and so disreputable in appearance that we were advised to try the King Edward Hotel; the MacDonald, the clerk said, was full up. Molson reported to the President of the University the next day that this experience at Jarvie had been the most interesting one they had had on the whole trip.

For several years Molson and McDonald wrote a round-robin letter to be read to all the friends they had made in the Jarvie district, and when Hugh Molson (now Sir Hugh Molson, M.P.), returned to Canada in 1936 on a visit, he spent a week with Roy Newnham at Jarvie, visiting the friends he had made years before.

Not all our experiences with English visitors were as happy as the Molson-McDonald episode. In the middle twenties scarcely a month passed without a visitor or a group of visitors from the British Isles. Many of them were interesting and pleasant enough, but every so often we entertained a real prize package in the person of a retired British general on his way home after years of pig-sticking in Poona, or an ancient explorer with an illustrated lecture on the flora and fauna of lower Patagonia.

One of these travelling representatives of the "Empah" we are not likely to forget. This was a typical comic opera British brigadier-general, with an illustrated lecture called "Some aspects of the war in the Middle East." He presented himself at my office on the afternoon before his evening lecture, corsetted, bemedalled and monocled. He had an attaché case in which he carried, wrapped in an old copy of the *London Times,* about 75 lantern slides. These he spread out on my desk and requested that we take charge of the lot and provide a projector and an operator for his performance in Convocation Hall that evening. Always on occasions of this kind H. P. Brown, our visual aids expert, was called upon to take responsibility for handling the show, and on this occasion he set up his biggest lantern in the centre aisle of the hall, using the stage curtain of the Convocation platform as his screen. The slides the Brigadier had left were a battered collection of coloured glass, unnumbered and without markings of any sort to indicate which was the top or bottom of the picture.

The lecture had been well advertised, and by 8 p.m. the hall was fairly well filled, mostly with people from the city. For over an hour, some two hundred bored Canadians listened to the most disjointed lecture ever heard in that auditorium. Our speaker stood in front of the screen with a billiard cue for a pointer and, with his monocle firmly fixed in his left eye, attempted to identify the pictures as they came along. In this he was rarely successful, and since the slides were not numbered in any sort of sequence we were jumped from Palestine to Gallipoli, to India, and back again to the near East. The talk went something like this:

"What have we heah? Oh yes, entering Jerusalem I think, Allenby on the left. Good soldier Allenby. Next slide please. Watering our horses, heah—next slide please. Heah we are in India. Sacred cows on the sidewalks, bit of a nuisance, but India's all right. No trouble in India. Next slide please." Thus it continued for over an hour. I sometimes think that this sort of stupidity was partly responsible for the signs one saw occasionally in the west, "No Englishmen need apply." At any rate they were not helpful in strengthening "the bonds of Empah."

6

Radio Station CKUA and the Radio League

IN 1926, OTTEWELL, with the backing of Dr. H. M. Tory, then President of the University of Alberta, succeeded in persuading the Provincial government to provide a grant of $5,000 for the purpose of building a radio transmitter for the use of the Department of of Extension. Ottewell's long experience with the problems and vicissitudes of pioneer life, not only as an extension lecturer, but as a youth on an Alberta homestead, had convinced him that radio could be used as a valuable medium for public education. There were many remote settlements in Alberta whose people were isolated, particularly during the winter, from all contact with the outside world. Ottewell believed that for purposes of information, education and entertainment, a University Radio Station could serve these people in a way not possible through the already existing commercial stations.

With the help of the Department of Electrical Engineering, Radio Station CKUA was ready to go on the air in the fall of 1927. H. P. Brown, who was the Department's expert on visual aids, was enthusiastic about the possibilities of the new gadget. I, as Assistant Director of the Department, was sceptical and slightly contemptuous of the whole undertaking. These were the days when bug-eyed enthusiasts would sit up half the night glued to their crystal sets, listening to the crash, bang, whistle, wheeze, of remote signals and report breathlessly to their bored acquaintances next morning "last night I got Texas." I had no radio of my own, but on various occasions when storm-bound in some village or farm house I had listened in nervous irritation to the evangelical bellowing of Mr. Aberhart (then principal of a Calgary high school and later the first Social Credit Premier of the Province) and had caught distorted, tortured bits of organ music from the Mormon Temple in Salt Lake City. I could see no use for such a treacherous medium. But the children of darkness are wiser in their generation than the children of light —I, of course, being one of the children of light—so Brown and Ottewell persisted in their enthusiasm and continued to experiment with a programme of recorded music, lectures on agricultural problems, short one-act plays, etc. It was not until 1928 when Ottewell became registrar of the University and I took over as Director of the Department that H. P. Brown was able to enlist my support for the expenditure of funds from our overworked budget to build a studio, install new equipment, and generally take an interest in what he rightly believed to be one of the most important educational instruments of all time.

Brown, who was in charge of CKUA operations, doubled in nearly everything. He was disc jockey, announcer, gave occasional lectures, and watched over the mechanics of broadcasting with an eagle eye. He was on duty about eighteen hours a day, because in addition to the care of CKUA he had charge of a visual aids department which boasted 800 sets of magic lantern slides and a film library of some 100 moving picture films which needed constant repairs and attention.

In an article published by H. P. Brown in January, 1955, he lists some of the "firsts" in the history of this pioneer station. "They had their own orchestra of twenty pieces; their own radio players; a wealth of lecture talent; one of the finest pipe organs in the country (the memorial organ in Convocation Hall) and the co-operation of student groups in debating, mixed chorus, opera and sports. University courses on radio included languages and the first broadcast of French lessons to the schools of a Canadian Province came from CKUA in 1928. Among other firsts was a provincial network of stations known as the Foothills Network, the first interprovincial hookup for university debates and sports, the first Citizens Forum (called the Round Table) alternating between Calgary and Edmonton, and the first transcontinental hookup, organized by the Canadian National Telegraphs of which CKUA was the Edmonton outlet."

Equipment for the station was crude enough, but the studio itself looked like an Arab's tent. It was all flapping burlap. Sound effects were invented on the spot. I remember showing H. P. how a good reproduction of the sound of a galloping horse could be made by tapping the fingers on the cover of a note book. Every passing car or barking dog penetrated the walls of the canvas studio and went on the air. On one occasion, says Brown, when a play was being broadcast dealing with the Indian mutiny, Jessie, watching from the walls of Lucknow exclaimed, "Hark, I hear the bagpipes." The control operator was not quite ready with the bagpipe record and the listeners distinctly heard a CPR locomotive crossing the high level bridge emit two long and two short blasts from its whistle.

Once we had invited Maurice Colborne (who was in Edmonton with a British company of actors presenting a repertoire of Bernard Shaw's plays) to deliver an encouraging address to the Alberta Drama League and the hundreds of Little Theatre groups throughout the Province. We had taken pains to let everyone know of the coming event and Colborne was assured of a very large listening audience. He had just nicely started with his talk when H. P. came to my office and whispered, "Holy smoke, we're off the air, I think we've blown a tube. What do we do now?" I said, "Just let him go on. What he doesn't know won't hurt him." Later I drove him to the theatre in time to go on stage. He never knew that he had been pouring out his soul to a dead microphone.

Actually it was Tyrone Guthrie who eventually convinced me of the tremendous possibilities of radio. I think it was in 1927 or 1928 that Sir Henry Thornton installed receiving sets in the club cars of the Trans-Canada trains of the CNR and shortly afterward engaged Guthrie, who was already widely known as a theatrical producer and had been successful in the production of radio plays over the BBC to come to Montreal as Director of programmes for the CNR. This was, I believe, the first attempt at a Trans-Canada network and the weekly plays Guthrie produced, some of them by the well-known Canadian writer Merrill Denison, during the winter of 1928-1929 were, from an experimental and public interest point of view, the most important developments in radio broadcasting up to that time in Canada. I shall never forget the dramatized story of Henry Hudson adrift in an open boat in Hudson's Bay and the sound effects of the ice-floes, the groaning oarlocks, the howling of the wind, the very feel of the cold and the despair of Hudson, played by Ivor Lewis, and his crew. It had the same effect on me as the Flaherty film, Nanook of the North, which, I think, was the first really good documentary film produced in North America and did much to demonstrate the possibilities of the film as an educational device. In the same way, Guthrie during his stay in Canada showed what a powerful medium the radio could be in the field of education.

Incidentally, it may be worth while at this time to tell of my first meeting with Tyrone Guthrie. After his winter's work was finished the CNR arranged a trip for him through Western Canada, and eventually I received notice from E. A. Weir, then Assistant Director of publicity for the CNR and in charge of their radio programmes, that Mr. Tyrone Guthrie would arrive in Edmonton on a certain date and would like to visit the University and see something of the work going on in the Department of Extension. One sunny, warm morning in July, I met the overnight train from Calgary and watched the passengers getting off, without any idea of what my guest looked like. I didn't know whether to look for "a tall man wi' a sporran, or a short man wi' a beard." After everyone had trailed off the station platform, there remained a six-foot-five giant in a rumpled summer suit, a white sports shirt, open down the front almost to the navel, sandals without socks, no hat, clutching an attaché case which was apparently all the luggage he possessed. I found it difficult to believe this was my man, but I approached and said, "Are you Mr. Guthrie?" "Yes indeed, and you, I'm sure, are Cobitt."

I took him to my house for breakfast, and afterward he wandered around the living-room looking at some Canadian paintings. Finally he came to a stop in front of three etchings by an English artist whose name I've forgotten. I said, "Well, how do you like them?" "Not

very good, you know, Cobitt, not very good." Afterwards I became convinced he was right, and the
etchings went down to the cellar and never reappeared.

I had arranged a reception for the afternoon at
Government House in order to give the Edmonton
Little Theatre crowd and others a chance to meet our
distinguished visitor. After we had met the President
of the University, Dr. R. C. Wallace, and had spent
the morning looking around, I took Guthrie home
for lunch at the Government House reception. There
were a hundred or more people present, and I recall
that when Mrs. Walsh, wife of the Lieutenant-
Governor, took Guthrie around introducing him to
the guests, Mrs. Balmer Watt, known to everyone as
"Peg," looked down at his feet, then slowly upward,
and gasped "My God, does it never stop?" Guthrie
joined in the laughter and all at once everyone felt
at home. For the next hour he charmed and fascinated
his audience with informative and witty stories about
the London theatre and his experiences in Canada.

This was the time when the Aird Commission
report was being discussed in the press and in Parliament, and Alan Plaunt had organized the Radio
League for the purpose of promoting the general idea
of public ownership of radio and specifically the
implementation of the Aird Commission recommendations. I became the Western representative of the
Radio League, and everywhere I went I carried copies
of the Aird report, propaganda literature released by
the Ottawa office of the Radio League, and whenever

there was an opportunity I attempted to get formal resolutions passed by responsible organizations supporting the recommendations of the Aird Report. In less than a year some fifty resolutions from farm organizations, women's institutes, boards of trade, church societies, etc., were sent from Alberta to the office of the Radio League in Ottawa as evidence of the interest already existing among Western people regarding the future of broadcasting in Canada.

There was perhaps a keener interest in radio in the rural areas of the West than anywhere else because of the long winter isolation of homesteaders and farm people generally. The absence of outside entertainment and news of the world and its happenings, market information, etc., made the western farmer more dependent upon radio than most people, and the concept of public ownership was at that time, particularly in Alberta under the Farmers' Government, more readily understood and accepted than in the eastern Provinces.

Alan Plaunt was a young Ottawa man of considerable wealth who had already demonstrated his consuming interest in public affairs as founder of the Young Canada Movement. This was an attempt to enlist young men and women in rural areas in an organized campaign for a keener and more enlightened interest in problems affecting Canadian life. It was a short-lived experiment, but during its lifetime won the devotion of a number of progressive young Canadians, many of whom have since become outstanding in their chosen fields—Orville Shugg, the organizer of the Farm Broadcast Department of the CBC and now Publicity Director of the Dairy Farmers of Canada; Leonard Harman, Secretary of the United Farmers Co-operative of Ontario; Ralph Staples, Director of the Co-operative Union of Canada; R. Alex. Sim, for ten years Director of Extension Services at Macdonald College, now with the Citizenship Branch of the Department of Citizenship and Immigration at Ottawa, to mention only a few. Alan was a dynamic person with enormous energy and indomitable courage. He was an inspiration to everyone associated with him and his tragic death in 1943 was a loss to the whole of Canada.

In organizing the Canadian Radio League, Alan Plaunt had in mind an organization which would carry the battle for public control of radio broadcasting in opposition to the strongly-developed lobby financed by the supporters of private control. In this effort he was joined by such men as Graham Spry, at that time Secretary of the Associated Canadian Clubs; Brooke Claxton, who had become well known throughout Canada as one of the founders of the Canadian League; Mr. (now Senator) Norman Lambert, and others; but the financial obligations of the undertaking were met almost entirely by Alan Plaunt. It was he who persuaded W. Gladstone Murray, then in one of the top positions of the BBC to come to Canada to look over the situation, meet with members of the government and recommend the procedures involved in the implementation of the Aird Report. I happened to be in Ottawa at the time of Murray's first visit, and it was apparent that his personal charm, his intellectual brilliance and vigour had in a few days made a very sharp impression upon everyone. Alan Plaunt and his associates were convinced that if, as, and when the corporation recommended by the Aird Commission was established Gladstone Murray was the man for its General Manager. The brief submitted by Murray, based on his own knowledge of Canadian conditions and his intimate understanding of the problems associated with publicly-owned broadcasting, did much to persuade the government and a large section of the Canadian public that the system outlined by the Aird Report was the right plan for Canada. It should be noted here, however, that Gladstone Murray's report did not recommend a public service monopoly. The underlying idea in his recommendations was a partnership between public and private radio, guaranteeing the general acceptance of social responsibility—a concept which was not acceptable to Alan Plaunt or other members of the Radio League.

Gladstone Murray was a Canadian, born in British Columbia. He had won a Rhodes scholarship from McGill in 1912, and after a brilliant career at Oxford had further distinguished himself in World War I, first in the infantry and later in the RFC. But when the first Radio Commission was established in 1933 Murray was not available, and the first General Manager was Thomas Maher, who was followed in

1934 by Hector Charlesworth. In 1936, largely due to the persistent agitation of Alan Plaunt and the Radio League, the Commission was abolished and the present Corporation established with Murray as its first General Manager and L. W. Brockington, Q.C., as first Chairman of the Board of Governors, positions both men filled with great distinction and to which they gave invaluable service.

Meanwhile CKUA had expanded its programme. In 1932 the Carnegie Corporation, in addition to the cash grant already received, sent us a very large record-player and a library of over 900 recordings of classical music—symphonic, choral, operatic. This enabled us to go on the air every evening with an uninterrupted hour of the world's greatest music, and as a result the station became something more than a source of information chiefly of interest to farm people. It began to acquire a large listening audience of music lovers throughout the Province and beyond. About this time too Miss Sheila Marryat came on the staff as Programme Director, and her CKUA Players were among the first in Canada to produce one-act plays regularly on radio. There were private stations in Lethbridge, Calgary and Edmonton, and in 1932, with the co-operation of Gordon Love, owner of CFCN in Calgary, Tiny Elphicke of the *Calgary Herald* station, and the Alberta Pacific Grain Co. at Red Deer, arrangements were completed for a regular exchange of programmes. These three stations carried a number of the University programmes, and a weekly exchange of recordings was worked out. In exchange for our records of classical music they sent to us at regular intervals shipments of recordings of musical comedies, jazz, hit songs, etc. To this arrangement we gave the high-sounding title The Foothills Network, one of the first provincial radio networks, I believe, in Canada. One of its most spectacular successes had been in the teaching of French, through conversational classes given two or three afternoons a week by Professor Hector Allard and Professor Edouard Sonet. In these classes were enrolled several hundred people, among them Mr. Justice Frank Ford, who gave credit to CKUA and his faithful attendance at its broadcasts for his fluency in French.

A prominent lawyer in Edmonton who owned an old set was unable to tune out CKUA, which was all across the dial. "I can't hear a darn thing on my radio except your ruddy French," he complained.

7

But Is It Education?

FATHER JIMMY TOMPKINS, the late famous founder of the St. Francis Xavier Movement, used to say: "In adult education you learn from the people you serve. It is the little men who make giants." We were always learning the techniques of our trade. The equipment we carried, the moving pictures, lantern slides, lectures, were useful as entertainment and as a means of persuading people to brave the rigors of the winter storms and bad roads in order to attend a meeting. But if the Extension man has nothing more in his repertoire than entertainment and pleasant talk, he won't accomplish much.

The old concept of university Extension as a series of lectures on such remote subjects as the foreign policy of Patagonia or Tennyson's Use of the Comma would be wildly out of place in a pioneer community whose people are, of necessity, interested in such mundane questions as fertilizers, soil surveys, how to winter fall pigs, how to organize and manage a co-operative or credit union, how to build a root cellar, fix a tractor, or build a community hall. That does not mean that there is no place in the extension programme of a Provincial university for the finer interests.

In my day in Alberta there were debating societies, literary and dramatic clubs in nearly every town and village in the Province. In addition to travelling libraries, we provided a package library system with carefully prepared material on over one hundred current problems for use by debating clubs. These were brought up to date every year and were widely used by Women's Institutes, Young People's Societies, Junior Farmers' organizations, High School Debating Leagues, and literary societies. In fact, for one year we had a member of the staff who gave all his time to judging debates and instructing in the art of public speaking. Every day's mail contained dozens of requests for material on subjects to be discussed at the next meeting of the society. Once, I recall, we received an urgent request for material on the question, "Resolved that it is better to have a dirty, good natured wife, than a clean, bad-tempered one." Oddly enough, the local debating club has now almost completely disappeared and given way to the much more effective discussion group in which everyone can have a part. But, back of all this, was the place of the expert, and the professors from the Faculty of Agriculture were in constant demand for practical instruction at the short courses we were beginning to organize throughout the country. Much of the best work of an Extension man however was accomplished, not on the platform, but in discussions in the homes of the people, following the school house meeting.

Once in 1924 I was asked to visit a pioneer settlement about 100 miles northwest of Edmonton. I started my journey about eight o'clock in the morning. It was in the latter part of June, and heavy rains had turned the roads into an almost impassible quagmire. On two or three occasions I had to be hauled out of mudholes, but at 5 p.m. I arrived at the small village which was my destination. On the front door of the little hotel, which was a Chinese restaurant with a couple of bedrooms upstairs, was posted a notice which read: "Dear Professor, the whole village has gone to the stampede two miles north. Come and join us."

I followed a well-worn wagon road north, and presently came to what was later to become a local fair ground. The stampede was in full swing. There was no one here, as in the Calgary stampede, to help a man off his horse after he managed to stay on board a few seconds; he had to ride the bucking maniac to a finish or be prepared to die in the attempt. It was wild and hilarious sport, but by 6 p.m. the fun was over and the crowd began to move in the direction of a big marquee tent where dinner was being served. I thought it was about time to make myself known, so I introduced myself to a large florid gentleman in a Stetson hat who seemed to be master of ceremonies.

"Sure glad you got here, Perfessor. I was afraid the way the roads are, you wouldn't make it. We're all looking forward to a good time tonight. Hope you brought along a big supply of films. This will be the first moving picture show ever seen in this district. Everyone is excited about it, especially the kids."

We sat down to a good meal, and as soon as we were all through eating my friend stood up and called for attention.

"The Perfessor is here and, as you all know, we're going to have a picture show in the community hall. But we got a little problem here. You all remember that Jimmie Law and his neighbour out west of the village got caught with a lot of wheat out last fall, and this spring, to keep it from rotting in the rain, we took the hall out there and piled the wheat into it. The grain was all shipped a few weeks ago but the hall is still out there. I want a half-a-dozen good teams to go out and bring her back."

There were plenty of volunteers, and an hour or so later the hall, which was on skids, came sailing majestically along what passed for a main street and was promptly jacked into place. By nine o'clock, an early hour in Western Canada, we were ready to proceed with the show.

I got out my 28 mm. machine, set up the twelve-volt battery, unpacked my films, and was all ready to go ahead, when I discovered that the lad who had packed the machine had neglected to include the crank. There was no possible way of turning that machine except with a properly fitted crank. I was in despair. I discussed the problem with the Chairman, who looked for a moment as though the world had come to an end. Then he said:

"Wait a minute, we've got a blacksmith here in the village. I believe he could make a crank for that machine." The blacksmith was paged, and after taking a long look at the thing, he said: "I think I can make do."

While he was away, I got the crowd singing; then I gave a talk about the University for about half-an-hour, all the time watching the door and praying for "Night and Blücher." Still the blacksmith did not appear. I recited almost a whole book of W. H. Drummond's French-Canadian poems (at which, by the way, I was pretty good). At last the door opened and the smith appeared triumphantly waving a crank. He had obviously been drinking, which explained his tardiness, but the apparatus worked like a charm. H. P. Brown tells me that crank has been kept in the Department of Extension as a memento of the early days.

That night I sat in a bachelor's shack in the village with half-a-dozen farmers and their wives, and before morning we had worked out the preliminary plans for a consumer's co-operative, which has since become one of the most successful in the Province.

Another incident is perhaps worth recording. W. D. Albright of Beaver Lodge, who was Superintendent of the Dominion Experimental Farm at that place, had arranged in 1930 for me to come to the Peace River country for a couple of weeks on a lecture tour. I often wonder if anything has ever been written about this remarkable man. He and his wife had gone up there by wagon train in 1891, and had by this time built up a Dominion experimental farm which served as a demonstration centre for field crops, livestock, small fruits, and even apple-growing, for that whole district, about 450 miles northwest of Edmonton. He was known and beloved by everyone from High Prairie to Pouce Coupe on both sides of the great river, the Peace, which cuts the country in two from west to east from Hudson's Hope to Peace River Crossing, where it turns northeast to join, 400 miles farther on, the Mackenzie waterways. There were at that time about 30,000 people in the Alberta section of what was known as the Peace River Block, and most of them would acknowledge that they owed more to W. D. Albright than to any other single individual in the north. Wherever he went he preached better farming methods, and "outside" (which was anywhere in Canada other than the Peace River country) he never tired of talking about the virtues of that lovely country and its people.

This visit I speak of was just at the time of the early spring of 1930 when the depression was at its worst. Most of my engagements were on the south side of the Peace River, along the highway running from Grande Prairie to Pouce Coupe. At that time the most famous "eating house" in all the north country was

Ma Brainard's place, about halfway between Grande
Prairie and Pouce Coupe—a distance of ninety miles.
Mr. Albright had planned our trip so that we would
stop there for lunch on our way to Pouce Coupe.

Ma Brainard's place was made up of a series of log
shacks built end to end along the highway and across
the road from a lovely little lake. She was a big,
bustling woman of about sixty years of age, with a
crippled husband a good deal older than herself.

We left Beaver Lodge in a howling snowstorm and
arrived at Brainard's about twelve o'clock. The place
was warm and cosy and the two tables down the centre
were loaded with food, but Mrs. Brainard welcomed
us with her customary greeting, "If I'd only knowed
yez were comin', I'd a had somethin' in the house to
eat." A meal at Ma Brainard's was something to talk
about. In a few minutes we were seated at a table
which already groaned with cold meats of every
description; but that was not enough. In from the
kitchen came a huge platter of boiled venison, a roast
wild duck, hot mashed potatoes and turnips and two
or three kinds of pie. During the meal Ma Brainard
pointed to a large framed photograph of Sir Henry
Thornton, whom she described as "the best eatin'
man" she had ever had in the place.

I was to appear in the Community Hall at Dawson
Creek the next evening, but the roads were so bad
Mr. Albright decided we would spend the night at
Brainard's and push on the following day. We left at
seven o'clock a.m. and drove through snow and mud,

arriving at Pouce Coupe in time for lunch; it was a distance of 45 miles. From Pouce Coupe to Dawson Creek is only about 15 miles, and we pulled in to the little hotel at the latter place about four o'clock in the afternoon. At that time Dawson Creek had a population of perhaps 200 people, with a small hotel, grain elevator, churches, school, community hall, a few shops and about 30 or 40 houses. Today, I am told, it is a modern city of 10,000. Mr. Albright left me there and drove on to Fort St. John, where he had a meeting of his own that evening.

I was sitting in the lobby of the hotel when the door opened and a tall, rangy Englishman of about forty years of age came over and sat down beside me.

"Stranger here?"

"Yes, I am."

"Thinkin' of takin' up land?"

"No, I'm giving a lecture in the community hall tonight."

"Oh." Long silence.

"Know anything about bugs?"

"Well, I've met a few bedbugs in my time."

"No, I mean, did you ever make a study of insects?"

"No, never."

"Well, I'm a bit of a whiz on bugs and what not. Just made a bit of money out of them's a matter of fact."

"Tell me about it."

"Well, its this way. I was born in Bristol, and as a schoolboy I made a hobby of collecting and mounting all sorts of insects. After the war I decided to come to Canada. My dear old mother was sure she'd never see me again. Canada, to her, was full of savages and the chances of survival were pretty slim. I came directly to Alberta; went broke on a Soldier Settlement farm south of Vermilion; and about five or six years ago I came up here and opened up a series of trap-lines north of Fort St. John.

"I had three or four cabins over a distance of about 75 miles and I worked them over regularly, living alone most of the time. I didn't keep much contact with the outside world, but I had always been a subscriber to the magazine *Nature,* and when I would get back to my base camp after a week or so out on my trap-lines, I would usually find a stack of mail and a copy of *Nature.*

"In one of these I saw one night an advertisement offering a price of $5,000 for a well-preserved and well-mounted collection of Arctic fleas. The advertisement was by a New York millionaire who was said to have the world's largest collection of fleas.

"I immediately sent off a letter asking for confirmation of the offer, and when I received it I replied that I would undertake the job the next winter.

"In the fall of 1929 I closed up my cabins, made my way up to Fort Reliance and built myself a cabin east of there on the Thelon River. I was after Arctic animals of any sort, particularly foxes, because they are just about the most productive flea-bags in the world. I caught plenty of fox, but I soon found out what I should have known anyway—that as soon as you trap a fox the fleas all desert his body and disappear.

"It happened that when I left England my dear old mother gave me a knitted burial shroud. I had used it as a blanket for so long that it had a fine human smell to it. So I rigged up a deadfall near one of my traps and folded the shroud into the bottom and sides of the hole. It worked all right. The fleas cosied up in the shroud and my troubles were over. Before the winter was gone I had a fine collection of fat fleas ready to send off to New York."

At this point he pulled out a bank book and showed me a deposit of $5,000. I'll never know, of course, whether the story was fancy bred or whether there was an element of truth in it.

That night after my show was over, a burly Englishman and his wife, whose names I have forgotten, invited me to spend the night at their place in the hills across the river from the town of Pouce Coupe. We left Dawson Creek at 10 p.m. and made our way in a Model T Ford to the banks of the Pouce Coupe River just below the town. There we left the car and embarked on a small cable ferry which carried us across the turbulent river, where we picked up another car of the same vintage and followed a winding trail up onto a plateau which overlooked the valley.

This was an amazing place. There was a long, low ranch house of red painted logs surrounded by about ten acres of cleared land. Inside, a fire was blazing in a big stone fireplace. The polished floors were covered with good rugs, and the walls were hung with a few good pictures, with here and there a coyote or bear skin. My hosts lived near London, England, during the winter months, but early every spring came back to their western home in time to look after a crop of strawberries, raspberries, watermelons, cucumbers, etc. They were obviously well-to-do people who had chosen this way of life, and, together with a hired man and his wife, remained on the place until November, when winter closed in. They sold their produce in Pouce Coupe and supplied the little Red Cross hospital in the village with fresh fruit all summer. Part of the fascination of the west is that one is constantly meeting people of this sort from other lands who have settled in the wilderness and made it blossom like the rose.

It was on a later trip to the Peace River country that I stayed overnight with a man who operated an extensive fruit and vegetable farm on the west bank of the Peace River, about ten miles below the town of Peace River not far from where the river turns northward on its way to the Mackenzie waterways. His name was J. B. Early, and he had come in the late 1920's from Idaho, where he had owned what he called a "stump farm." He had been burned out several times in Idaho, and finally decided to look for a place where the constant threat of destruction from forest fires would be, at least, remote. He had found what he wanted on that rich stretch of land along the western side of the Peace River just below the town which slopes downward in an easterly direction to the river's edge.

On the high land of his property a small spring-fed lake emptied into a creek which bordered the north boundary of his land. In the event of a drought he could divert water from the creek and thus irrigate the lower part of his acreage. I suspect that many of the people in the district considered the man daft when he announced that he intended to grow fruit of all kinds—watermelons, muskmelons, red and black currants, gooseberries, in fact all types of small fruits —on part of his land, and the rest would be devoted to the production of fresh vegetables for the local market. Early had been on his land about six years when I first visited his place and already he had become a legend. It was September, and out in the fields there were a dozen or more women gathering the crop of cucumbers, young corn, beets, turnips and other vegetables. He told me that he had very little packing or shipping to do, because on week-ends trucks came from all over the Peace River to pick up his produce. The week before I was there he had sold three tons of cucumbers, and the buyers had picked them themselves, fresh from the field.

He was in demand constantly at Women's Institute meetings and Farm Organization conventions, and he had already had a profound influence upon the farm people along the north shore of the Peace River— through Fairview and on to Fort St. John. Most of the farmers were producers of wheat and coarse grains, dairy products and beef cattle. There was never much time for flower gardens, home beautification or raising fresh vegetables. A man was lucky if he had time for such staples as potatoes and turnips.

Mr. Early told me that some years after he had settled on his land he had planted a large flower garden along the western boundary of his farm, just where the highway passed on its way to the bridge crossing the river into Peace River town. He said he used to watch the farmers and their wives, on their way into the town on Saturdays, stop their wagons or cars and gaze in wonder at the blaze of colours from his wide variety of blooms. The women remembered the flowers around their old homes in the east, and here they were in profusion: sweet peas with blossoms the size of a silver dollar, roses, dahlias, enormous chrysanthemums and tall, varicoloured gladioli. It wasn't long, he said, before flower-gardens and fresh vegetable plots began to appear around the farm homes of the Peace River country.

Early had built himself a kind of primitive dug-out hothouse on the bank of the gully and here he grew seedlings of all sorts in the early spring ready for transplanting later on. He was an inventive genius, and had made arrangements with the local liquor vendor to save for him the papier mâché boxes in which certain brands of Scotch whiskey were encased. These he cut in cross-sections about three or four inches square and used as tiny crates for his seedlings. I don't know whether this modern pioneer ever made a fortune but he must have done very well from his enterprise, and he was known and respected throughout the north country.

It was on that trip that I met a farmer, near the mouth of the Smokey River, who in addition to his regular farming operations was experimenting with the raising of mink. He told me he thought he could work out a scheme that would give him 100 per cent. profit on his pelts. He proposed to build two big wire cages side by side. In one of them he would keep cats and in the other minks. He would skin the cats and feed their carcasses to the mink, then skin the mink and feed their bodies to the cats. As he remarked, it sounded feasible, and he thought he'd take a go at it as soon as he got around to raising some extra cats.

8

We Have With Us Tonight

ANYONE who has spent the greater part of a lifetime in talking to groups of people in schoolhouses, community halls and church basements, as I have done, is bound to have many vivid memories not only of people and places, but of amusing experiences. I recall stormy nights in Alberta when my audience consisted of only three or four people who had braved the cold and the snowdrifts to hear me, and two or three occasions when the local chairman and I sat alone beside a roaring fire in some crossroads school and spent an evening in talk because we had no audience at all.

I put on a show one night in a Negro schoolhouse near Athabasca Landing. This was a small community of coloured farm people, an offshoot of a much larger Negro settlement west of Edmonton. A young Negro schoolteacher presided at my meeting, and before she introduced me she read the latest issue of a weekly newspaper which she produced herself on a battered old typewriter. Two of the news items produced roars of laughter.

Last week Mrs. Reg. Wilson went on a visit to Edmonton. While she was away she left her young chickens in the care of the Lord, and when she came home they were all dead.

The other day Biff Andrews bought himself a pint of squirrel whiskey. Then he went to the bush and was seen trying to climb a tree backwards. The reason for the celebration—a nine-pound baby boy.

Once I gave a lecture in a small town in the cattle country of Southern Alberta. The subject was Mark Twain's Life and Works. It was supposed to be amusing, and certainly the audience seemed to enjoy it, but after the lecture was over, a tall raw-boned English woman, who looked as if she had just ridden a bronco in from the nearest ranch, walked up the aisle, looked me straight in the eye and said, "That was a perfectly stupid leckchah."

My best memories, however, have to do with introductions. The professors at the University of Alberta had a formidable collection of these, gathered from extension lecture trips in the early days.

Professor E. K. Broadus, head of the English Department, used to tell of going to a town not far from Edmonton to give an illustrated lecture on Shakespeare. When he got off the train he saw that the main street of the town was decorated with big red signs which read: "Come and hear Professor Broadus lecture on Shakespeare, and enjoy yourselves afterwards at the dance."

Once I gave a talk in the auditorium of a Methodist church on Wednesday night after the regular prayer meeting. Before my part of the programme began the Minister said, "I always open these meetings with prayer," and during his petition he said, "Oh Thou, who alone canst perform mighty works, inspire the speaker of the evening."

One of the best of my introductions was also in a small Alberta church. The Minister, who had been a classmate of mine at McGill University, introduced me at considerable length and finished his remarks by saying, "I can assure you Mr. Corbett is a veritable Mount Vesuvius, and without further remarks I will now allow him to erupt." Some one at the back of the hall spoke up. "Hot air, I suppose." Once I was introduced to a convention of women by a lady chairman who said, "Our speaker today, needs no introduction; his name is a household word in Alberta. I have much pleasure in introducing Mr. Crawford."

But when all of our stories of introductions were told, Ottewell had the best. He was lecturing one night in Southern Alberta at a time when the government was distributing strychnine for gopher poison. Ottewell's meeting was called for the double purpose of hearing him speak and distributing the strychnine. After Ottewell finished his talk, the chairman got up and said, "Now yez have all heard the lecture. Any of

yez that want strychnine come up and get it." Ottewell
used to say, "They all came up too, mind you."

That story had an amusing sequel. A good many
years later I was invited to attend a convention of the
Alberta School Trustees' Association and give a
demonstration of the use of visual aids in teaching.
The meeting was held in Central United Church in
Calgary, and there were upwards of 500 delegates in
attendance. H. P. Brown had gone to Calgary the day
before the conference was to begin and had set up a
moving picture machine equipped for sound in one
aisle, a small 16 mm. machine for classroom films in
another aisle, and in a third aisle a film-strip projector.
On the platform he had set up a radio receiving set for
use in schools. The programme was arranged so that
he could use one instrument after another, the whole
demonstration to be concluded in an hour. This was
the year when the question of the larger school unit
of administration was being discussed by rural communities all over Alberta. At this conference it was a
major item on the agenda. I was to appear on the
platform at 11 a.m., and as I explained the function
and uses of each of the machines H. P. Brown would
run through a sound film—a silent 16 mm. film—
demonstrate the film-strip projector, and last of all
tune in a school radio programme.

I had agreed to address the Calgary Kiwanis Club
immediately following my appearance at the Trustees'
Conference, so I was anxious to get our demonstration
started on time. When I arrived at the church audi-

torium, however, there was a furious debate going on over the terms of the proposed legislation implementing the larger unit of administration plan. The Chairman, Dr. Staples of Stettler, was having great difficulty keeping order.

At 11.15 I sent a note up to the Chairman, reminding him that our programme was scheduled to start promptly at 11 o'clock, and that I had another engagement at 12. I watched him read the note, and then he picked up a gavel which looked as though it had been designed for driving fence posts. He pounded on the pulpit until he got attention; then he said, "According to the programme we are now to hear Mr. Corbett of the University give a demonstration of visual aids. Do you want to hear him or do you want to put him off." With one voice the delegates shouted, "Put him off." But just then a little man ran up the aisle, jumped on the platform and shouted, "I came all the way from Milk River to see this demonstration and I say let's hear the University fellow now." There was a chorus of boos, and once again the Chairman used his huge gavel. "We'll put it to a vote. Those of you who want to hear Mr. Corbett stand up." Quite a crowd stood up and were counted. "Those of you who don't want to hear him stand up." Again they were counted. I won by a count of two heads.

This put me in a very difficult position, so I began by telling them Ottewell's story of the strychnine. Then I said, "The only difference between you people and the crowd in that little schoolhouse that night is that those people knew when they wanted their poison and you don't." Everybody had a good laugh and our show went off very well. During my talk I noticed a stout red-faced man in the front row, who kept on laughing over the strychnine story. When I left the auditorium this man followed me to the door, put his hand on my shoulder, and said, "I just want to tell you that I am the chap who presided at Ottewell's meeting night, but I never knew till now that I'd made such a good joke."

One of the places I loved to go was the home of Henry and Zella Spencer at Warwick Farm, near the town of Edgerton, which is on the CNR main line east of Wainwright. Henry and his brother Herbert had homesteaded here sometime around 1909, and when I first visited them in 1925 they were farming, I think, close to 1,000 acres, mostly in wheat. It was a precarious business and over and over again the crop would be lost to hail, drought or some sort of insect pest. But it was a fascinating home where repeated disappointment had been unable to defeat the inherent gaiety and overwhelming goodwill of its inhabitants. Henry was to become later a leading member of the House of Commons, one of that unforgettable coterie known as The Ginger Group, led by J. S. Woodsworth, whose place in Canadian parliamentary history will remain one of the most distinguished in the record of the Canadian people.

At this time the two men, Henry and Herbert, were

leaders in the United Farmers of Alberta, and Zella, Henry's wife, was most active in the sister movement, the United Farm Women of Alberta. In addition they were in the forefront of every movement in the community designed to improve the living conditions of the neighbourhood. My first appearance in Edgerton district was a disastrous affair. Arrangements had been made for a moving picture show and lecture at a local schoolhouse a few miles from the Spencer farm. I was met at the Edgerton station by Herbert Spencer driving an odd-looking team made up of a tall rangy mule called Ella (I was always making the mistake of calling Mrs. Spencer 'Ella' and the mule 'Zella') and a squat little pony. It was in February and the roads were heavy with snow.

The train from Edmonton was late and it was 7 p.m. when I arrived. The meeting was scheduled for 8.30, and we had about nine miles of drifted snow to plough through to the schoolhouse. Herbert stowed all my equipment in the back of the "cutter" (in New Brunswick this sort of vehicle in my youth was called a "pung") and we started. About five miles from town the cutter turned clean upside down and we were thrown out in the snow. Herbert and I were discussing some weighty issue at the time, and I suppose that is why, when we got the sleigh righted and back on the road again, we neglected to look in the back to see what had happened to the moving picture machine, the films, the slide projector and boxes of slides.

It was nine o'clock when we finally arrived at the

school where an impatient audience of men, women and many children who had come to see their first movie greeted us with loud applause. Herbert told me to go on up to the platform to be introduced while he unloaded and set up the twelve-volt battery and the moving picture machine. I was in the midst of acknowledging the very kind introduction of the chairman and the applause of the audience when Herbert came up to the platform and with a stricken face announced that all our equipment had disappeared, and he could only conclude it had all fallen out when we upset on the way from Edgerton. He suggested that the meeting proceed while he and a neighbour returned to the spot where we had lost our load. Unfortunately some good Samaritan passing by had picked up the whole issue and taken it home. Somehow we got through the evening, but it was a sad and disappointing introduction to a community which was magnanimous enough to invite me back many times, and where I later had many happy days.

Incidentally the hotel at Edgerton in those days had the reputation of being the coldest spot in Alberta. Two stories were told of that famous hostelry which may be worthwhile recording here.

Two commercial travellers who had spent the night in the hotel were having breakfast in the dining-room one bitterly cold morning, when a farmer who had just driven a load of wheat into town appeared in the doorway. His beard was coated with ice and his eyes were almost frozen shut. As he passed the travellers one of them looked up in astonishment and said, "My God, which room did you sleep in?"

The other story is one that has been a subject of controversy for many years. The incident is reputed to have occurred in several different places in the west. However, I heard it told about the much-maligned hotel in the village of Edgerton. The train to Edmonton used to go through Edgerton at about 5 a.m., and it was the custom for commercial travellers who wished to return to Edmonton to sleep half-dressed so they could make a quick dash to the station when the train whistled far down the track. One cold morning a traveller just managed to swing onto the end of the last car as the train was pulling out of the station. He was half-dressed and carried over his arm a heavy overcoat and various articles of wearing apparel. Also wrapped up in these garments was the water pitcher from the hotel room. He put this carefully down on the seat. His companions looked at him in amazement and said "What's the big idea, bringing along the water pitcher?" "Had to," said he, "my teeth are frozen in it."

However, these were events of long ago, and I'm told that the Edgerton Hotel is now a model of comfort.

One of the most embarrassing experiences of my sixteen years in Alberta as a wandering minstrel took place in a small village not far from Macleod. It was on July 1st, 1924, at the time when the town of Macleod celebrated its fiftieth birthday, and some

15,000 people paid admission to the Stampede ground to see enacted again the stirring drama of the early days when Fort Macleod was the North-West Police centre for what is now the Province of Alberta. The three days of the celebration were marked by such brilliant scenes as the west may never see again. The historical pageant which was the main event of the opening day was a sight not soon forgotten. A detachment of Mounties led the procession, and was followed by a long line of Indians in full tribal costume and war paint. There was the old stagecoach which used to run from Fort Benton to Macleod. A pony mated with a cow drew a rickety wagon of 1874. A whiskey trader with two barrels of hooch strapped to his vehicle passed along amid the cheers of the crowd. And then, sitting straight in their saddles with a seat which belied the white hair under their pill-box caps, came all that was left of the men of the N.W.M.P. of 1874. All Alberta seemed to be there, statesmen, cowboys, Indians, showmen, ranchers and men of every profession. I was present at this carnival for the reason that the Women's Institute of a nearby crossroads village wished to take advantage of the celebration to help pay for the new community hall which had just been opened. They knew they could be sure of a large turnout, because every hotel and stopping place for miles around was filled with ranchers and cowboys.

It was the custom of the Department of Extension to distribute every year a list of available films and slide lectures to voluntary organizations everywhere in the Province. That year there were a number of new films, among them a two-hour biblical documentary called A Prince of the House of David. In the letter inviting me to come and give an evening of film entertainment, the women had asked for the usual number of short comics for the children and, as the main attraction for the grownups, they asked for The House of David. I thought at the time that this was a strange choice, but in looking into the matter afterwards I discovered that somehow the notice sent out had listed the film simply as The House of David. It happened that that year and for some years afterward a bearded baseball team called The House of David had been barnstorming in Western Canada, taking on local teams and in most cases beating them outrageously. They were not only brilliant performers on the baseball diamond but gave exhibitions of trick baseball which were extremely funny. Everywhere huge crowds turned out to see them.

On the night of my show, the new community hall was packed with cowboys and local baseball fans. For the first half hour all went well, as I ran through a couple of short comics for the children. Then came the main feature film, and as the shepherds with their sheep appeared on the hills of Judea there were gasps of dismay and low mutterings among the crowd. As soon as it became apparent that the film had nothing to do with baseball, but with a section of Old Testament history, the audience began to dwindle away, and after a half hour of the film had been shown there were only the children and the disgruntled members of the Women's Institute left in the hall. Needless to say, I made no charge for this disastrous demonstration, but that was poor consolation for the good people who had promoted the undertaking.

9

Carnegie Grant

IN 1931 the University of Alberta had a visit from
Dr. Learned of the Carnegie Corporation of New York.
The work of the Department of Extension had received
a good deal of attention by this time. One visiting
educationalist from Great Britain, whose name I've
forgotten, referred to it in a speech before the
Montreal Canadian Club as "the most interesting
educational experiment" he had seen anywhere. One
of the by-products of Dr. Learned's visit was his sugges-
tion to the President, Dr. R. C. Wallace, that the
University might submit to the Corporation a request
for assistance in the development of a fine arts programme—music, painting and drama—to be adminis-
tered by the Department of Extension.

Accordingly, with much prayer and fasting, two
plans were submitted, one of which called for the
expenditure of $15,000 a year for three years, and

another budgeted at $10,000 a year for the same period. In both cases the plans outlined called for the appointment of a full-time instructor in dramatics, the provision of highly qualified adjudicators for the Alberta School Musical Festivals, already well established throughout the Province, and the circulation of art and handicraft exhibits to schools and adult organizations.

The first of these, i.e. the appointment of a full-time instructor in dramatics, was perhaps the most important part of the plan and would absorb fifty per cent of the total budget. The reason for this was that the depression had closed most of the small-town moving picture houses, and the people outside the larger cities had been more and more thrown back on their own resources for entertainment. The result was the growth of hundreds of small dramatic or little theatre groups. A great many of these, particularly in the villages and rural communities, knew very little about choosing a play or how to stage it. Plays chosen were often such inane and worthless scripts as Deacon Stubbs of Perkins Corners, or similar drivel. It had been obvious for some time that if the Department of Extension was to give adequate direction to this movement a qualified director was needed, and we had already added to our staff Mrs. Elizabeth Sterling Haynes, a graduate of the University of Toronto, who had for some years played a distinguished role as an actress and producer in the Alberta Drama League.

The second part of the plan was to assist in the

direction and development of the Alberta School Musical Festivals. This was a quite remarkable programme, organized and directed by the Provincial Department of Education, and had been established in co-operation with local school authorities in three main divisions — Southern, Central and Northern Alberta. Programmes were drawn up and printed by the Department early in the year, and distributed by district committees to all the school teachers in the area. There were prizes in choral and solo singing and in instrumental work for all grades. Prizes were also offered for prescribed readings and recitations.

I remember adjudicating the elocution entries at the Vegreville Festival in the spring of 1931, when the winner, high school section, was a young Ukrainian lad of sixteen, with ragged sweater and patched trousers, who electrified all of us with his rendition of Mark Antony's speech from Julius Caesar. It was a moving experience and served to demonstrate the potential educational value of the scheme.

The Festivals were usually held in the largest town or village in the district, and lasted two or three days, usually in the month of May, and the winners later would proceed to take part in the Provincial Festival. One of the weaknesses of the programme was the lack of first-class adjudication, and our hope in the Department of Extension was to use one-third of whatever grant of money we received from the Carnegie Corporation to pay the fees and expenses of highly qualified adjudicators in all the festival districts.

The third part of our plan seemed to a good many people pretty far-fetched. Our general idea in planning such an overall programme was roughly as follows. The Brownlee Government, which was a "farmer government," was doing all in its power to meet the economic problems of the people of the Province. Nothing could be done about the collapse of prices for farm produce; this condition was world-wide. But assistance was being given through government relief agencies. It seemed under such circumstances that the role of the University Department of Extension, under a greatly reduced budget, was to do everything in its power to support those voluntary agencies already in existence designed to sustain the morale of the people, particularly in rural areas.

Our budget had been reduced, but we derived considerable income during the years from a charge for services. A picture show cost the community $10.00, which included the out-of-pocket expenses of the operator; a lecture series cost $5.00 per night, and by arranging a series of shows or lectures covering two weeks or more at that rate the trip could be made to pay for itself; rentals on films, slides and projectors provided another source of income. So we operated on an overall budget of about $35,000. This provided for ... the salaries and operating expenses of a staff of some fifteen people, including clerical assistance. When the depression was at its worst our Provincial grant was reduced again, and the people in rural areas were no longer able to pay the nominal fees for these services. We then decided to have no set fees for moving picture shows or lectures, but to depend upon a collection taken at the end of each picture show or lecture. So our work went on, and strangely enough, in spite of the impoverished condition of the people, they rose gallantly to the occasion, and the collections usually met the costs of the enterprise. Our appeal to the Carnegie Corporation for additional funds was based on the belief that with a little assistance we could continue to expand our activities. In the spring of 1932 our request for a grant of $10,000 a year for three years was approved by the Carnegie Corporation and we prepared to develop our programme.

There was an active Alberta Artists Association in the Province and a well established branch of the Canadian Handicrafts Guild. In co-operation with the latter two organizations, arrangements were made to carry out the third part of our project.

With the assistance of the late Dr. W. G. Carpenter of the Calgary Technical Institute and his students, a truck was built for the purpose of carrying exhibits of pictures and crafts to the small towns and rural community halls of the Province. Loans of pictures were made by the National Gallery, the Alberta Artists Association, and through the good offices of Professor James Adam, Professor of Drawing at the University of Alberta, a loan of fifty pictures from the Glasgow Art Gallery was added to the collection. For three winters these pictures were shown in community halls, church basements, or wherever a suitable place could be found in the small towns of Southern and Central Alberta. We had a man to drive the truck, and he was accompanied by Major Norbury of Edmonton as lecturer. There was no charge for this service other than accommodation for the driver and lecturer and a suitable place to hang the exhibit.

The show was usually sponsored by a local organization. The children of the elementary schools were asked to attend in the mornings, the high school students in the afternoons, and the general public at night. Stands of two or three days were arranged, sometimes a showing for a longer period, depending on the size of the town or village. With rare exceptions the hall was crowded all day with successive classes of school children, and at night people drove miles across the windswept prairies to see the pictures and listen to the illustrated lecture. Some of these meetings were deeply moving. Once, in Southern Alberta, a show was given in a community hall far from any town or village. It was a crossroads centre, with a school and a general store, an elevator and two or three houses. It was a cold, blustery night, but the hall was packed with people, many of whom had driven ten or fifteen miles over the treeless countryside. One woman wrote to the Department: "I came here from Surrey, England, twenty years ago and I think I had forgotten until that night how much beauty there is in the world."

Major Norbury, who was a painter of considerable

note, was constantly on the lookout for school children with artistic gifts, and when painting classes were started at the Banff School of Fine Arts in 1934 we had three young students who were sent to the school on small scholarships provided by a school district which had been visited by the art exhibits the previous winter. One of these children, a girl of sixteen, came from a farm south of Medicine Hat. Her people were very poor and the child arrived wearing patched jeans, a boy's shirt and scuffed sneakers. This youngster was the most promising pupil of the year, and later sold some of her pictures to such distinguished collectors as Lady Tweedsmuir and R. B. Bennett. Some years later I heard she managed to win a scholarship which took her to London to study. But I've lost all track of her and have even forgotten her name.

These were the activities made possible by the Carnegie money, and which led up to the organization of the Banff School of Fine Arts.

10

The Banff School of Fine Arts

IN THE SPRING of 1933 the Alberta Drama Festival was held in Lethbridge, with Mr. L. W. Brockington as Adjudicator. I happened to be President of the League that year, and it was my duty to introduce Mr. Brockington on the opening night. I made use on that occasion of a bon mot which was not original with me. "Mr. Brockington," I said, "would be a kind and understanding adjudicator; he had been brought up in a Christian home and was a firm believer in the Biblical injunction 'Let him that is without sin stone the first cast.'" The joke fell flat on its face. If anyone in the audience got it they were not amused, for there was not even a ripple of laughter.

But it didn't take Brockington long to warm them up. In his opening remarks he said that what the American theatre needed most was "nasal disarmament." When this brought a roar of applause he immediately pointed out that it is easy to sin in the other direction: "When I listen to some English actors I never know whether they are annoyed or adenoid." He spoke of the influence of the American theatre upon Canadians and such organizations as the Alberta Drama League. This was to be expected because the influence of our great neighbour to the south was affecting every aspect of Canadian life. Those were the days of Canadian prohibition and international bootlegging. In fact, he said, we have for years engaged in a game of international hop-scotch with the United States in which "we've done most of the hopping and they've got all the scotch."

I mention the Alberta Drama League and the Lethbridge Festival because it was during this meeting that the plans for a training school in the theatre were first discussed. Elizabeth Sterling Haynes had been on our Extension staff as Instructor in Drama for nearly two years and had held regional short courses for the leaders of little theatre groups all over the Province. Shortly before this the Alberta Drama League had, for competitive purposes, organized the Province into three main divisions—the Peace River, Central and Southern Alberta districts. The plan was that each division would hold a regional drama festival in February or March and the winning group would then proceed to take part in the provincial festival in Edmonton, Calgary or Lethbridge, which was usually held late in April or the first week in May. In the winter of 1932-1933 Mrs. Haynes had held local training courses in all of the regions, and had discovered that there were something like three hundred small drama groups in the Province, all needing help in choosing plays and in such matters as casting, costuming, lighting, directing and general stage-craft. We had a large selection of one-act plays available in the library of the Department of Extension. There were also many books on production. But it became clear that a summer school in the theatre arts was greatly needed. Mrs. Haynes had discussed the problem with me on various occasions, and when we went to the Lethbridge Festival we had a tentative plan drawn up, with Banff in mind as the best possible place for the experiment.

It was decided that we would present the idea at the annual meeting of the Alberta Drama League, which was to be held on Sunday morning immediately following the close of the festival on Saturday night. At the meeting Mrs. Haynes told of her work throughout the Province and of the many struggling little drama clubs, some of them doing excellent work, but all in need of training and general assistance. I then outlined our plan for holding a summer training school at some such place as Jasper or Banff during the coming summer, and asked for the approval and support of the Drama League. After a good deal of discussion the Executive decided not to participate in the experiment. There seemed to be a pretty general opinion that the idea was premature and there was the danger that the League might find itself involved financially in a venture that was doomed to failure.

When we returned to the University I discussed the matter with the President, Dr. R. C. Wallace, and the Extension Committee, which was composed of Dr. John McEachern, Dr. W. G. Hardy, myself and the President. Dr. Wallace pointed out that the Institute of Pacific Relations was meeting at the Banff Springs Hotel that summer and there might be difficulty in getting sufficient accommodation, but if we could overcome physical problems of that sort he would give the plan his approval and authorize the use of $1,000 from the Carnegie Grant to finance the undertaking.

I immediately drove down to Banff and discussed our proposal with the school board, service clubs, and members of the town council. They were all keen on the idea and promised every possible assistance. There was a rather shaky old theatre just across the bridge and facing the Bow River, known as Brett Hall (after the famous Dr. Brett, founder of the Brett Hospital and later Lieutenant-Governor of Alberta), which was used by the local Little Theatre and was equipped with work-shops, dressing rooms, stage, curtains, etc. This would be placed at our disposal, and the school board agreed to allow us the use of the public school and high school for classrooms, library and general centre for the students, the only charge being for janitor services.

Meanwhile a publicity campaign was set on foot, and Mrs. Haynes got together a collection of twelve one-act plays, in a huge mimeographed edition to be made available to students at a price of $3.00. We decided upon a registration fee of $1.00, and as far as possible to arrange with tourist cabin owners to reserve tentative accommodation for forty or fifty students. I was perfectly certain that none of those likely to attend could afford to stay at the Banff Springs Hotel, but I took the precaution of reserving some additional rooms at the smaller, less expensive hotels. We expected at the most a registration of about 75 people, but on the opening day nearly 200 turned up. Our staff consisted of Mrs. Haynes, Ted Cohen, a young Edmonton lawyer who had already distinguished himself as a producer, his brother Elliott, an experienced and skilful stage craftsman, Gwyllim Edwards of Calgary as Registrar and Treasurer. I think our greatest surprise was that, while the students who registered that first year came mostly from the four Western Provinces, there were also one or two from Eastern Canada, one from the United States, and one by some odd chance from Australia. The school is now world famous, but even in its first year it had a slight international flavour.

I don't suppose any group of amateur actors ever performed before such a distinguished audience as a picked group from the school did one night, when three one-act plays were produced for the entertainment of the Institute of Pacific Relations. Among the people in the audience at the Banff Little Theatre that night were two members of the British House of Lords; delegates from Japan, China, Australia; the

Prime Minister of New Zealand, Walter Nash; a vice-president of General Motors; Mr. Luce (just beginning to be known as publisher of *Time* and *Fortune*) ; E. A. Carter, Secretary of the I.P.A., and many other noted people whose names I have forgotten.

One incident that first year we all recall with great pleasure was the presence at the school of a farmer and his wife from Saskatchewan. The man was about sixty years of age, his wife perhaps fifty. They had driven the 500 miles from their farm, near the little town of Marshall, in a battered old Model T. Ford— the first holiday they had had in thirty years. They had a tent, bedding and cooking equipment, and they set up their establishment somewhere on the side of Tunnel Mountain. At first no one noticed them. Then one day, after one of the lectures, they came forward and offered their services. The man was a skilful carpenter and was at once put to work making stage sets, and his wife to helping with costumes. They were a quiet, dignified and extraordinarily handsome couple, and were soon popular with students and staff.

One day about a week after the school opened they handed Mrs. Haynes a one-act play they had written. They were very hesitant about it, afraid it wasn't much good, but would she read and criticize it for them. I think it was called Defeat, and it depicted life on a Saskatchewan wheat farm during the depression. Mrs. Haynes and Ted Cohen were so enthusiastic about its possibilities that they decided to produce it on the closing night, when a number of plays written by students were to be presented. The man and his wife were cast as the father and mother, and I think the only other members of the cast were a son and daughter, picked from the student body. It was such a success that it was later entered in the Saskatchewan Drama Festival and was chosen to represent that Province at the Dominion Drama Festival in Ottawa in the spring of 1934, where the author and his wife were awarded a prize for one of the best Canadian plays, and very high praise for their acting.

The summer of 1934, the second year of the School, we had on our teaching staff, in addition to our own people, four who gave the school its first promise of the international stature it has since achieved. These were Roy Mitchell, his wife, Jocelyn Taylor, Wally House, all of New York University Drama Division, and Joseph Smith, Professor of Speech from the University of Utah. There were also Mary Ferguson, wife of G. V. Ferguson, then of the *Winnipeg Free Press,* who taught Eurythymics. A. C. Leighton and H. G. Glyde, noted artists, were in charge of the classes in painting.

All of these were able, competent teachers, but I will be forgiven if I make special mention of the contribution made by Roy Mitchell, Jocelyn Taylor and Wallace House. In addition to his class lectures in the Theatre Arts, Roy Mitchell gave lectures which were open to the public two or three evenings a week. These covered the whole range of his activities in the theatre, from the days when he was Director of the Hart House

Theatre through his Broadway experiences and his work as head of the Drama Division of New York University. He was a man of enormous gusto and good-natured cynicism, and his lectures were an experience few of his students will ever forget.

But I think that the sessions at the 1934 School which will live longest in the memories of those who attended were the classes in folk singing led by Jocelyn Taylor and Wally House. They were both accomplished guitarists and their repertoire of folk songs represented every part of North America and many European countries. They were a joy to students and public alike.

The Banff School, under the direction of Donald Cameron (now Senator Cameron), who took over when I left Alberta in 1936, has become an institution of international reputation. It offers a much wider choice of subjects than it did in the early days. It is now more than a summer school. Its magnificent dormitories, class rooms, and work-shops have made it an all-year-round training school and convention centre, and it has become one of the major cultural centres in North America.

11

Transition

MY SIXTEEN YEARS in Alberta were the happiest
and most exciting years of my life. To begin with, I
loved my work. I was constantly on the move, meeting
new people and new problems. The fact that we had
available within the university a wealth of information
which could make life fuller and more satisfying for
everyone provided me with an outlet for my inherited
missionary instincts.

Besides, one was caught up and exhilarated by the
spirit of change which lived like wine in the air in
the early twenties. In politics, the old line parties had
almost completely disappeared when the farmers took
over the Provincial government in 1921. Scientific
research and experimentation in every phase of agriculture was being encouraged. Advances in educational
standards and techniques were in progress. Farm
organizations (the United Farmers of Alberta) were

in the forefront of every movement for the improvement of living conditions for farm people. Following the meteor-like campaign headed by Aaron Sapiro of California, the big producers' co-operatives began to take shape in the three Prairie Provinces.

This spirit of change was not confined to Western Canada. The growth of national feeling following World War I was finding expression in the development of such national organizations as The Associated Canadian Clubs, The League for Peace and Reconstruction, etc. A group of young Montreal intellectuals led by Brooke Claxton in 1925 organized the Canadian League, and within a few years affiliated groups were formed in most of the western cities. Later, I think in 1928, the Canadian League was absorbed by the Canadian Institute of International Affairs.

Speaking of those days in a letter to the writer recently, the Hon. Brooke Claxton said, "Every kind of organization, national and local, cultural and religious, political and commercial was at a peak of activity hardly equalled since. This was also true of art. I remember having the first showing of the Group of Seven to be held in Montreal at my house in 1927. All these were manifestations of the growth of national feeling—it was nationwide, spontaneous, inevitable. It cut across political, racial and social lines. Indeed it was curiously a-political."

There were of course many people of the old school who looked with fierce disapproval upon this new birth of national sentiment, among them Mr. R. B. Bennett, who in 1927 was elected leader of the Conservative party. At a meeting of the Associated Canadian Clubs in Calgary in 1928 Mr. Bennett came out strongly against nationalism. In a dinner speech before the delegates assembled from all parts of Canada he said, "Canada is as nothing without the little grey islands in the North Sea. This talk of Canadian Nationhood is dangerous nonsense. Canadians are British first, last and all the time."

But the years between 1925 and 1929 were golden years in the Canadian West, and it was good to be in it and part of it.

The depression which struck with such devastating force in 1929 was a crushing setback to the faith and the aspirations of western people. In the early thirties thousands of farm families in Alberta were forced to apply for Government relief. Many of my friends who in 1926-1927 looked forward to years of continued prosperity were reduced in 1930 to desperate privation.

I remember walking one September night with a farmer friend through a half section of his stooked wheat. It was a lovely sight in the moonlight. Threshing had started that day and the yield was averaging forty bushels to the acre, but every bushel of it would send my friend deeper into debt. The crop had been touched with frost and the grade was low. The best price he could get at the local elevator was fourteen cents per bushel. Looking across the Pembina river at the homestead of his nearest neighbour, my friend said, "Jimmy Brett across the river there had more sense than I; he didn't put in a crop at all this year. He and his family of six are on relief and his kids look better than mine do."

Meanwhile a high school principal in Calgary by the name of William Aberhart had read a little book on social credit written by the English actor, Maurice Colborne, and all at once he saw a new heaven and a new earth. This was not an uncommon experience for Aberhart. He was apocalyptic by nature. Once in 1925 I went to the town of Lloydminster to give a lecture in the Presbyterian Church. As I sat in the hotel lobby waiting for the minister to take me to my appointment, I could see crowds of people moving in the direction of the town hall. I asked mine host, the hotel owner, what all the excitement was about. He said, "They's a chap come up here from Calgary, name of Aberhart; he's goin' to talk about the end of the world; Armageddes he calls it. Seems like next June down there in the Black Hills of South Dakota all the righteous are going to be gathered together and in one fell swoop they're goin' to be taken up to heaven. Well sir, that's where the crowd's movin' right now. They sure want to get in on that hay-ride. Me, I'm goin' to be down there next June with the rest of the boys, but I'm goin' to have a hot-dog stand. They's goin' to be a lot of hungry people around the day after Armageddes."

I think I had about fifteen people at my lecture. Next morning at breakfast there was great excitement in the hotel dining-room. It seems that the night before, Aberhart in his speech had referred to Greece as one of the seven horns of the beast mentioned in the Old Testament. The hotel cook, an enormous Greek who had once been a professional wrestler, apparently had jumped on the platform, arms waving and demanded an apology from the speaker.

Even at that early date, Aberhart had his Bible Institute in Calgary, and could be heard every Sunday on the radio preaching his gospel. By the time he had discovered social credit there were very few people in Alberta who hadn't listened to him at some time or another, and of course everyone had heard of him.

The times were therefore ripe for Aberhart's campaign in the early thirties. There was great want and privation in the land. It was not so much a question of food. People could in most localities get enough to eat, but mothers were concerned about the health of their children, youngsters needed glasses, their teeth fixed; they needed clothing if they were to be able to continue at school. There was no money for even the barest necessities of decent living. Then Aberhart began to talk on the radio and at public meetings about social credit. He promised $25.00 a month for every adult in every family in Alberta. He was a man of God; surely he could be trusted to know what he was talking about.

It was Aberhart's custom when addressing a crowd of people to hold aloft a cheque for say, fifty dollars, and he would explain that he had signed that cheque in payment of a bill a month before. It had gone the rounds, completed its mission and was now back in his hands again—just a piece of paper. "Fountain-pen money" he called it.

I referred this question of fountain-pen money to an old friend of mine. I quite honestly wanted to understand social credit but it was then, and has remained, completely beyond my comprehension. So I asked 7.U. Brown to enlighten me. 7.U. was so called because his cattle brand was a U with a 7 in it. He lived west of High River, where he operated one of the finest cattle ranches in Southern Alberta. He lived with his two charming spinster sisters, and their home was a delightful place to visit. 7.U. had a habit of speaking in parables. So when I asked him about Aberhart's fountain-pen money, he began in his usual way. "Well," he said, "I'll tell ye. It reminds me of a feller that came in here to this country the same year I did. That was in 1891. This feller came here from South Dakota, and he took up land just south of my place. But as long as I knew him that feller never done nothin' on his ranch but put up prairie hay. He had good land, mind ye, but he couldn't be bothered raisin' any crops. So one day I was passin' his place and there he was out on the land, and as usual he and his men were stackin' up hay. So I says to him I says, Bill what in the name of God do you do with all the hay? Well, he says, what's wrong with hay? It's a good crop ain't it? I says yes, it's a good crop, but what do ye do with so much of it. Well, he says, I feed some to my cattle,

I sell some in High River and come to think of it, my neighbours take quite a lot of it away. Well, I says, do they ever pay you for it? No, he says, I can't rightly say they do. Well, I says, you must lose a lot of money that way. No, he says, I ain't never lost any money, but I lost a hell of a lot of hay. That's Aberhart's idea of money; it ain't even hay, it's just nothin'."

Once I went with a group of friends to hear Aberhart speak. It was in the Edmonton Arena in 1934. We were fortunate in having seats on the floor of the Arena, quite close to the raised platform from which Aberhart was speaking. By this time he commanded huge audiences wherever he went, and the Edmonton Arena was packed. During the course of his remarks Aberhart complained about the press coverage he was getting. He exorcised the people who criticized himself and his economic theories, and at one point he shouted, "Anyone would think a man has to be crazy to understand social credit." A drunk a few seats ahead of us couldn't let that opening pass, so he shouted, "Well, by God, it would help."

In any case this was the man who in the Provincial elections of 1935 swept the Farmers' Government out of power and took over the government of the Province.

There followed during the next year a period of utter confusion. People began at once to demand the $25.00 a month they had been promised. Doctors and dentists in small towns were besieged by mothers who had driven into town with their children seeking treatment of all sorts and promising to pay as soon as the first monthly $25.00 came along.

At the university there was some anxiety on the part of the staff concerning the future of the institution. It had not been very long before he became Premier that Aberhart had denounced the university as a "Godless institution." As a matter of fact, we were not interfered with in any way. The new government had plenty of more pressing problems than what was going on at the university.

But changes were also taking place at the University of Alberta. In 1936, Dr. R. C. Wallace, who had succeeded Dr. H. M. Tory as President of the university, was offered and accepted the Principalship of Queen's University. At the same time I was invited to become the first Executive Director of the newly formed Canadian Association for Adult Education.

It was to be for one year only, and I looked forward to returning to Alberta and my work there at the end of that time.

As matters turned out, I never got back to that lovely country again except for occasional visits.

By the end of my first year as Director of CAAE it was obvious that—to use a Canadian colloquialism—I had a tiger by the tail on a down-hill pull, and the rest of this story will be, I fear, a highly personal history of that organization.

PART TWO

12

New Horizons

IN AUGUST, 1936, with my wife and family, I moved to Toronto, which was to be the headquarters of the new organization. My daughter Joan, fourteen years of age, entered Bishop Strachan School. Paul, nineteen, who had already completed three years in Arts at the University of Alberta, entered his final year at Trinity College. Bruce, twenty-two, who had finished his B.Sc. course in engineering and was employed on the city engineering staff in Edmonton, we left behind; later the same year he also came to Toronto and proceeded towards his M.Sc. in Mining Engineering at the University of Toronto.

Thus we all started life again in new surroundings, and I embarked upon the most difficult task I had ever undertaken—to create from a document of aims and purposes a national institution dedicated to the idea that continued learning throughout life was not only possible but necessary if democratic institutions were to survive.

The story of the inception of the Canadian Association for Adult Education has been told over and over again and in many places. It is perhaps enough at this point to state that the idea of such an organization originated with W. J. Dunlop, who was then Director of the Extension Department of the University of Toronto and is now the Honourable Dr. W. J. Dunlop, Minister of Education for the Province of Ontario. From the beginning he had the support of Sir Robert Falconer, President of the University of Toronto, and Principal W. L. Grant of Upper Canada College.

Two national conferences had been called, one in 1934, which met at the University of Toronto, and another at Macdonald College, St. Anne de Bellevue, Quebec, in June, 1935. From these conferences, attended by delegates from every Province in the Dominion, emerged the CAAE with charter, constitution and bylaws and a starting budget of about $10,000. As briefly as possible, these were its objectives: To promote the development and improvement of adult education in Canada and to co-operate with similar organizations in other countries. So far as Canada was concerned its main function would be to serve as a clearing-house and co-ordinating agency for the hundreds of voluntary and official organizations at work in the field of adult education.

For the first winter's operation Mr. Dunlop provided me with an office in Simcoe Hall and the part-time services of one of his secretaries, but actually I had very little use for an office or a secretary during my first year as Director of CAAE. It became apparent to me at once that while there may be ivory towers in the academic world this was not one of them. It was my job to give blood and bones to an idea.

This meant that as soon as possible I must get to know the people in the universities and departments of education in every Province in Canada who were already at work or interested in adult education. It had been agreed at the first full-scale annual meeting of the Association, in October, 1936, that for the first few years the emphasis in our work should be on rural adult education. At the meeting called by Mr. Dunlop in Toronto in June, 1934, a provisional committee had been set up to carry forward the organizational work of the association. At the first meeting of the provisional committee, which was held at the University of Montreal, Dr. W. L. Grant urged that a survey be made of all the adult education activities in Canada, and added that an unnamed donor had provided a sum of $3,000 for the purpose. It was then agreed that the survey should get under way at once with one investigator for the Maritime Provinces, two for Quebec, one for Ontario, one for Manitoba and Saskatchewan, and one for Alberta and British Columbia. By the late fall of 1934 the survey had been completed, and during the winter of 1934-1935 the reports were edited and compiled by the late Dr. Peter Sandiford.

It was obvious from this report that the rural areas of Canada were in most Provinces the have-nots in adult education services. Also in the fall of 1936 the Dominion Bureau of Statistics published a report on library services in Canada which revealed the appalling fact that in some Canadian Provinces 90 per cent of the people living in rural areas were beyond the reach of ordinary library facilities. Since this put us on a par with the hill-billies of the Southern States so far as educational opportunities were concerned, it was perhaps natural that the council of the association should be unanimous in its decision to devote its efforts mainly to this area of Canadian life.

I started the first of my trans-Canada pilgrimages in October, 1936. In Prince Edward Island, Bramwell Chandler, then provincial librarian, and John Croteau, a young professor of economics at St. Dunstan's College in Charlottetown, were literally burning up the heather with a programme of adult education whose main function was the organization of credit unions and consumers co-operatives among the fishermen and the farmers of the Province. In this work they had the support of Monsignor Murphy, principal of St. Dunstan's College, the Departments of Agriculture and Education of the Province, the Catholic clergy of the Island, Colonel Keith Rogers, owner of radio station CFCP, and many other influential people on the island. The programme of work laid out for themselves by these two young men would have killed ordinary individuals. When they were not organizing and helping to run short courses, or keeping up with a regular weekly radio programme, they were out at night lecturing and organizing in country school houses all over the Island. In addition they had their regular work to do.

I had written to Chandler and Croteau suggesting

that I would like to meet them and see their work, and all arrangements had been completed; but when I got off the Island ferry at Borden and was met by the two men, I got the impression that so far as they were concerned this was just another "one of those things." They had had other visitors—to look at the library set up (P.E.I. was then the only Province with complete library coverage), report on their credit union work, etc. Perhaps I was unduly sensitive because I knew from my own experience in Alberta what a nuisance V.I.P.'s can be. However, they had decided to make what use they could of me, and for the next ten days I was kept on the go.

Every night we left Charlottetown, packed like sardines in the front seat of Bram Chandler's library truck. Croteau was an enormous man, six feet, four inches and weighing about 275 pounds. With Chandler in the driver's seat, myself next, and Croteau crammed in on the right side, we somehow managed to get the door shut. October can be a wet month on P.E.I. and this was before the roads were hard surfaced. Night after night we sloshed and slithered through the red mud on our way to remote school houses or community halls. The routine was always the same. Croteau would give a pep talk on Co-ops and Credit Unions, after which Bram Chandler would introduce me as the speaker of the evening. I only had one speech, which dealt in as sprightly a manner as I could manage with the significance of adult education; its necessity in a functioning democracy; its rewards in bettering standards of living; and as a medium for the enrichment of life. Night after night with stoney faces Chandler and Croteau bore up under this shattering experience. It has always been my custom, rightly or wrongly, to brighten such occasions with an apt story or illustration, but after the first attempt I gave up the idea entirely. Any attempts at humour were met with profound suspicion if not contempt.

I remember thinking at the time of Harry Lauder's first visit to Montreal in 1909. My landlady, who was a Highland Scot, went to hear one of his performances, and next morning at breakfast I asked her how she liked the show. "Oh," she said, "it was'na too bad, mine ye, but I had an awfy time to keep from laughin'." These people had no trouble refraining from mirth; they just resented foreigners and their so-called humour.

One of the most exciting experiences of the P.E.I. pilgrimage was our visit to Tyne Valley, my father's first congregation[1], where I had lived from the time I was three years of age until I was nine. When it was learned that one of "the Corbett boys" was to speak in the Presbyterian Church hall, the congregation turned out en masse. It was a heartwarming occasion. There were many people in the audience who remembered my father and mother, and as is the custom in that part of the country had kept track of the family and its various members ever since we had left the village, some forty years before. I think this was the first time I realized sharply that I was no longer young.

[1]See *Father, God Bless Him*, The Ryerson Press, Toronto. 1953.

The chairman, a tall man, stooped and gnarled by long years at heavy farm labour, who looked to be at least sixty years of age, shook my hand until I thought the bones would break, and said, "Hallo Eddie, remember me? I'm Jim Miller—you and I sat on the same double bench in the old schoolhouse."

That evening I stayed at the home of Mrs. Dan Forbes, who had been one of my mother's dearest friends, and late into the night she told me stories of the old days. Of the time I fell off the counter in her husband's store into a tub full of eggs. Of her son and myself breaking into Dan Forbes' warehouse, when we sat on a pile of dried apples and stuffed ourselves with the delicous chewy fruit until almost bursting and then washed it all down with a pint of molasses; the results were appalling and embarrassing, and Dr. Long had to be called on to minister to the terrible stomach cramps we suffered.

The next day I was taken to the old manse where we had lived for six years and where two members of the family were born. There the young minister showed me the records of the church kept by my father during his ministry. One entry I noticed in my father's fine handwriting was dated May 24, 1890, and read, "This day, the birthday of our beloved Queen Victoria, was born my first daughter. We intend to call her Jessie after her mother's only sister. Bless God for all His gifts."

The P.E.I. trip was a stimulating experience, and since the enthusiasm and vigour of the movement in P.E.I. stemmed from St. Francis Xavier and the philosophy of Father Jimmy Tompkins, Dr. M. M. Coady, and A. B. MacDonald, it made me all the more anxious to visit Antigonish and see for myself the work going on there; but this was an experience I was not to have until a year later.

After leaving P.E.I., I travelled to Saint John, where the late Dr. Fletcher Peacock, then Principal of the Technical Institute in that city, had made arrangements for me to address a joint meeting of the Board of Trade and the Canadian Club. Afterwards we drove to Fredericton. The Premier of the Province, Mr. Dysart, had invited me to appear before the Legislature, which was then in session. This was, in anticipation, a terrifying experience, but actually turned out to be very pleasant. I stood on the Speaker's dais, and on my right was the liberal majority, and on my left the small and rather grim conservative opposition. This was one of the first legislative assemblies in Canada, and some of the bewhiskered gentry looking down on me from their gilt-framed portraits dated back to the latter part of the 18th century. I think I must have made an impression, because shortly after that Dr. Fletcher Peacock was appointed Deputy Minister of Education and initiated a programme of school building designed to provide for rural areas a type of consolidated school which would serve as community centres equipped with every facility for adult education activities. Throughout his lifetime, Fletcher Peacock was a member of the Executive of CAAE and one of its most ardent supporters.

There followed then a trans-Canada safari, with

meetings and many speeches in Quebec City, Montreal, Winnipeg, Regina, Saskatoon, Calgary, Vancouver and Victoria. On the trip through the west I was accompanied by Drummond Wren who was then National Secretary of the Workers' Educational Association (WEA). At that time the WEA had branches in most of our Canadian universities, and Drummond Wren was a member of the first Executive Committee of our Association. There was then and for many years afterwards a close relationsip between the WEA and the Canadian Association for Adult Education, and on this particular trip through the Western Provinces, while Drummond was busy mending his fences, I was attempting to set up some of my own.

In Winnipeg we were entertained by the Manitoba Association for Adult Education, where Drummond spoke of the work of the WEA, and I told the meeting about the newly-organized national association. This was as it should be—the two national adult education organizations were working out their problems together, as they had done in Great Britain and elsewhere. In Vancouver however, I think we more or less cancelled each other out. The meeting there was arranged by Robert England, who had recently been appointed Director of Extension for the University of B.C., and my old friend, Brigadier Sherwood Lett (now Chief Justice of B.C. and Chancellor of the University). A luncheon meeting had been planned and we met in the very posh Pacific Club looking out over Vancouver Harbour. Quite a number of influential and wealthy business men attended, and Drummond and I were to speak briefly about the work we were trying to do. I spoke first, and made a plea for their encouragement and support of CAAE, its objectives and its dreams. Drummond Wren was a very forceful and witty speaker and not the least bit ashamed of being a militant socialist. He spoke very strongly about the need for better labour-management relations and the part the WEA could play in bringing this about. In doing so he took some hearty cracks at the kind of business man who feared that education would have an unsettling effect upon working people. It was all pleasant enough, but I had a feeling that our listeners were not deeply impressed with either of us.

It was a wearing but on the whole a profitable experience, and we arrived home a week before Christmas, 1936, exhausted but convinced that we had at least made a start with the foundation work of a national organization.

The rest of the winter of 1936-1937 was spent entirely in Central Canada. We started our magazine *Adult Learning,* with Mrs. Adelaide Plumptre as our first editor, and I began to work regularly with affiliated organizations in Montreal, Ottawa, Hamilton, London, and other centres. Gradually people began to discover that there was a central clearing-house for adult education, and before the summer of 1937 had arrived the demands upon my time became so pressing that I was at work night and day. Most of it was talk, endless talk. In Alberta people took the Department of Extension for granted. It was a branch of the University, and they had a right to its services.

Now, I had to explain to everyone what the Canadian Association for Adult Education was and what it was for.

Since I was away from the office most of the time, it was fortunate for the Association that we had as secretary Miss Jean Hoshal, now Mrs. Walter Willis, a graduate of the University of Saskatchewan, who was one of the most competent executives I have ever worked with. From 1927 till 1941 this young woman gave the new organization order and a measure of stability. Also, wherever I went I found that ministers and deputy ministers of education, university presidents and university directors of extension were eager to co-operate with us in every way. But most of all I was grateful for the never-failing kindness and loyalty of W. J. Dunlop. In every crisis of the first years, and there were many, I could depend on his strong support. It seemed to me that from coast to coast I had the encouragement and personal goodwill of everyone connected with education. I suppose this was natural enough, since our National Council was made up of representatives of the universities and departments of education of every Province in Canada.

It became apparent to me before the end of my first year of office that my chances of returning to Alberta at the end of a year were slim indeed, so I sent in my resignation and Donald Cameron was appointed Director of the Department, a position he filled with great distinction until 1956, when he resigned in order to give all his time, outside his duties as a Senator, to the Banff School of Fine Arts.

13

The Men of St. Francis Xavier

IN 1937 I received an invitation to take part in the Rural-Industrial Conference at St. Francis Xavier University. By this time the dramatic story of the successful rehabilitation programme of St. F.X. had spread throughout the English-speaking world, and every year the University was swamped with visitors from all over Canada, the U.S. and abroad.

If my memory serves me correctly there were some 600 delegates at the 1937 conference. A caravan of automobiles loaded with Baptist clergy and laymen, all of whom were involved in some way with the co-operative and Credit Union movements, had come from the mid-western United States. There were also present a great many clergymen, both Catholic and Protestant, including four Catholic Archbishops from the United States, and the Moderator of the Presbyterian Church of Canada. There were government

officials and business and professional men, but the
bulk of the attendance was made up of miners from
Cape Breton, and fishermen and farmers from Nova
Scotia, Prince Edward Island, and New Brunswick.
The programme was planned, directed, and for the
most part chaired by leaders in the co-operative and
credit unions of eastern Nova Scotia, which was the
territory in which the professors of St. F.X. had worked
out their ideas.

Doctor James Tompkins, better known as Father
Jimmy, had been the pioneer in the St. F.X. experiment, and I had met him on two previous occasions.
In the winter of 1927 he had called me by telephone
from the Macdonald Hotel in Edmonton. It was on a
Sunday morning. He had the day to spend in the
city on his way to a convention somewhere on the
Pacific Coast, and he wanted to have a look at our
department. I picked him up at his hotel and we
spent the day looking over our equipment and services.
I showed him our library with its open shelf section
and the piled up boxes of books ready to ship to
remote sections of the Province, our collection of films
and slides; the Radio Station, and the big map on
which we kept a record, by means of coloured pins, of
the communities we served from the Peace River to
the Montana border, and as best I could I answered
his questions about our programme of lectures, short
courses, etc.

I think he was impressed with the fact that close
to half a million people in the Province were using

or were at least exposed to our services. But at the end of the day I remember he told me of the poverty of his people and the necessity of helping them first to discover and develop by their own efforts whatever economic resources were available to them. The average income of a Nova Scotia fisherman, he said, at the very best might be three or four hundred dollars a year. Their children were undernourished; the schools were neglected and in many instances badly taught. The young people were leaving the country, and a way must be found to improve their standard of living before considering libraries or picture shows. "It's no use," he said, "talking to a man about his soul until you've put a shirt on his back and food in his belly." He was then about 56 years of age, with a thin wiry body, sharp features, piercing blue eyes, terrific physical energy and the expression of a medieval saint.

The next time I met Father Jimmy was at a conference of Adult Educators held at the University of Maine in Bangor. This was in July, 1937, and by that time his fame had gone abroad and he was constantly surrounded all during the conference by delegates from the United States. I was fortunate to get a few minutes with him, and it was for me a memorable occasion. We were walking across the Campus when a robust and over-enthusiastic Adult Educator with a perverted sense of humour caught up to us and took over the conversation. Among other inane remarks, he said, "I understand, ha, ha, that you are making

good Catholics of all those Nova Scotia fishermen."
This was the wrong thing to say to Father Jimmy.
For years he had been telling his co-operatives,
"There's no such things as a Catholic Co-operative
store, a Methodist store or a pious store—two plus two
makes four in the accounts no matter what your
religion may be."

Now he looked coldly at the ebullient American and
said, "God help us man, can you tell me any Catholic
way of canning lobsters?"

I was to meet him again many times, and spend long
hours with him, before he died in 1952. But now, at
this conference at St. F.X. only a few weeks after I had
met him at the University of Maine, I could see that
he was still looking me over and searching for a judg-
ment. When my turn came to address the conference,
Father Jimmy, Dr. M. M. Coady and A. B. MacDonald,
the three great leaders of the St. F.X. movement, sat
in front of me.

I suppose there were six or seven hundred people in
that hall, but those three were the only people I saw.
I was terrified. In a way it was like "preaching for a
call" in a Presbyterian church. I not only wanted, I
needed the approval and respect of these men and their
associates. Somehow I got through that speech. It
was lunch time and when I finished my talk everyone
turned his back and made for the nearest exit. I
slipped out a side entrance and made my way towards
the dining-room. I was sure I had been a complete
failure. I had forgotten that in the Maritime Provinces

people don't rush up to a speaker the moment he is through talking, grasp him warmly by the hand and say, "That was a REAL treat." Usually they just file quietly out of the building and say nothing at all. Of course, if a man happened to have been born in the Maritimes and was fairly well known, one or two people might wait for him outside the door and say, "Yon was a grand text ye had; too bad ye didna make a sermon out of it," but that would be about all.

But on this occasion I received an accolade I could never afterwards forget. Just as I was entering the dining-hall, Dr. Coady caught up to me. He put his arm around my shoulders and leaning over from his great height he said, "Father Jimmy thinks ye'll do."

The personal friendship of these three men during the next fifteen years was a constant inspiration to me, and their contribution to the Association and its work can never be over-estimated. There is no need to go into the history of the St. Francis Xavier experiment at this point. A dozen books and hundreds of articles have been written about it. In Dr. M. M. Coady's *Masters of Their Own Destiny* (Published 1939) and Prof. Alex Laidlaw's new book *The Campus and the Community* (D. Ed. Thesis, 1956) the story is told by two of the people best qualified to do so.

Dr. Tompkins had resigned from the University in 1921-1922 and had worked out his ideas in actual practice, first in the little parish of Canso, and later at Reserve Mines, Cape Breton. In 1928 the Department of Extension was established, largely through the efforts and the prodding of Dr. M. M. Coady and Dr. Tompkins, and nine years later, when I first visited the University, its work was, as I have stated, known everywhere.

Father Jimmy from his parish house in Reserve Mines continued in close co-operation with Dr. Coady, head of the Department of Extension, to inspire and direct the expanding programme of the department. But from the early 1930's on till his retirement in 1950, Dr. Tompkins began to turn his fiery zeal in new directions. He was getting old and a little weary, but there was much yet to be done. For twenty-five years he had been pushing, needling and sometimes maddening government officials, the clergy, the university authorities, and anyone who would listen to him about the sad plight of the Nova Scotia fishermen, miners and farmers. With endless patience he had helped to shepherd his "little people" towards a fuller measure of economic freedom. Of one thing he was now quite certain: the time had come to "close the gap between the man and the book." So he started a library.

"It's the people who make giants. Give them ideas and they'll blow the roof off. Get knowledge and nothing can stop you." This was the way he talked now, and with nickels and dimes he started the library in Reserve Mines which bears his name today.

Then his persistent digging into records got him started on another job. He discovered that it was possible to borrow on 25-year mortgages at 3½ per cent. from the Nova Scotia Housing Commission. So he got his people together to study, plan, and eventually build the first group of modern co-operative houses, now called Tompkinsville. I was at Reserve Mines staying with Father Jimmy when the first of the houses had been completed. They were two-storey buildings, with living-room, dining room and kitchen on the first floor and four bed-rooms and a bathroom on the second. This was in 1938, and $28.00 per month looked after interest and amortization. This was only the beginning. There are now some 400 of these co-operatively built houses.

Meanwhile, under the leadership of Dr. Coady and A. B. MacDonald and their many dedicated associates, the work at St. Francis Xavier continued to grow. These two men had come to their Kingdom for such a time as this. Coady was the thinker and philosopher. MacDonald was the man of action. Dr. Coady had been trained for the priesthood, and after graduation from St. Francis Xavier had taken his Ph.D. and D.D. in Rome and further graduate work at the Catholic University of America. Then he came back to his beloved country as Professor of Education at St. F.X. "If Dr. Tompkins was John the Baptist of the Antigonish movement, Dr. Coady was its St. Paul."[1] A. B. MacDonald had graduated from the Agricultural College at Guelph, Ontario, and became a competent and enthusiastic inspector of livestock. But Father Jimmy had had his eye on A.B. ever since he had

[1]Professor Laidlaw.

taught him philosophy as an undergraduate at St. F.X. He was convinced that one of the many things rural Nova Scotia needed was school inspectors who knew something about agriculture. In 1925, as a result of Father Jimmy's prodding, A.B. returned to his native heath as a school inspector. Actually his school inspecting was only a part of his assignment. He was far more used to prodding bullocks than school teachers. He spent every night holding meetings and trying to start a revival for better schools, better teachers, better equipment and co-operatives to pay for them. The next five years were great years for A.B., what with building new schools, organizing school gardens, school fairs, and study clubs, and lecturing at the Truro Normal School, he declared that he made such a nuisance of himself that everyone breathed a sigh of relief when Dr. Coady collared him in 1930 to be his assistant in the recently established Department of Extension at St. F.X.

For the next twenty years it was A.B. and the men who worked with him who gave hands and feet to the ideas of Coady and Tompkins. Both Coady and Mac-Donald were powerful platform speakers. A.B. was a genius at stirring an audience to immediate action. Coady would send them home to think for weeks about the things he had said. He would, for example, take them quickly over the historical processes by which since the Industrial Revolution men had lost what he called their "consumer rights." Then he would light up the whole picture with an unforgettable illustration. "Suppose," he would say, " a man wants to build a smokestack 150 feet high. In laying the foundation his workmen are careless and allow it to get out of plumb. The mistake is scarcely visible to the naked eye at first. When the stack is at 30 feet it is clear that it tilts a little, but it is still firm and the building goes on. But by the time it has gone up 150 feet it has become a dizzily leaning tower. The very builders are afraid of it. It is an ominous threatening thing. They hasten to prop it up. Long heavy wires are anchored in the ground and attached to the stack, but it is still unsafe; the whole structure will have to be rebuilt to put it back into plumb. The economic smokestack we have built in the last 150 years is just such a leaning memorial. In the beginning an error was allowed to creep in and the structure rose at an angle that grew more and more apparent as time went on. When the people awoke to a realization of their peril, they ran for the guy-wires to hold up the leaning tower. The various hand-outs and pensions, unemployment insurance and the rusty old wire of the dole were prominent, but the ugly thing they had allowed to grow out of their control now hangs over us all, a threatening monstrosity."

Speaking to a conference of teachers or educational officials he would challenge the very foundation of the accepted philosophy of education: "Our educational system has been for too long a convenient trap-door through which the bright people escape from the lowly callings into which they were born to the nice jobs at the top. We have stressed the thought that there is room at the top for everyone. There never was a bigger lie. In our educational process the common people have been left behind, and have come to believe that education is not necessary, since they are not cut out for the jobs in business and the professions. Thus we are left with a great vacuum in the minds of the masses. Nature abhors a vacuum. Sooner or later the tornadoes of revolution will blow in there, as recent history shows. We have to find a way to pump life back into these lives. That is the only answer to revolution and instability."

To the accusation that the St. F.X. approach to adult education was a materialistic approach, he would say, "Give us time; what you have seen is only the beginning. We have no desire to create a nation of shopkeepers whose only thoughts run to groceries and dividends. We want our people to look into the sun and into the depths of the sea. We want them to explore the hearts of flowers and the hearts of their fellowmen. We want them to live, to love, to play and pray with all their being. We want them to be men, whole men, eager to explore all the avenues of life and to attain perfection in all their faculties. Life for them shall not be in terms of merchandising, but in terms of all that is good and beautiful, be it economic, political, social, cultural or spiritual. They are the heirs of all the ages and of all the riches yet concealed. All the findings of science and philosophy are theirs. All the creations of art and literature are for them. If they are wise they will create the instruments to obtain them. They will usher in the new day by attending to the blessings of the old. They will use what they have to secure what they have not."

A. B. MacDonald, on the other hand, would bring them down to earth with a straight from the shoulder talk challenging his listeners to get together and get working on their organizational work. Once, when he was addressing a group of miners in a Cape Breton mining community, he was disturbed by a dozen or more men who had come into the meeting carrying a case of beer. He knew well enough that a sharp reprimand might lose him the meeting; so, still talking, he walked down the aisle to the back seats where the gang had settled, helped himself to a bottle of their beer, then walked back to the platform, knocked the neck off the bottle on the edge of the table, took a long drink and continued his speech. There was no more disturbance.

I first saw A.B. at work at a short course for fishermen which had been arranged by Monsignor Murphy, who was then Principal of St. Dunstan's College in Charlottetown, in January, 1941. On the second day of the short course one of the worst snow storms in the history of the Island blocked all highways and sideroads with drifts of snow which in some places were over ten feet high. After the third day of the storm not a car could be moved on the sideroads. A.B. had to get back to the mainland for another engagement, so Father McNeil of North Rustico arranged for a horse and bobsled to transport A.B. and his associate, Miss Ida Gallant, from North Rustico to Hunter River, eight miles away, in the hope that he could there catch a train to Borden. The story of that trip is too long to tell in detail here. They left at 5 a.m., and it is known that an hour later A.B. raided a farmhouse and emerged with woollen stockings for their half frozen feet. The horse had given up the struggle after three miles, and in a country where Paul Bunyan stories grow fresh every winter A.B. is described as striding into Hunter River at 9 a.m. carrying the horse on one of his gigantic shoulders and Miss Gallant under the other.

One other incident will serve to illustrate the physical prowess of A.B. Once at the end of a long morning's work in his office, A.B. and I started to drive from Antigonish to Moncton where he was to address a mass meeting of co-operators. The meeting was scheduled for 8 p.m. and we left Antigonish at 3 p.m. It was late in the fall, but the roads were good and by 6 o'clock we were approaching the town of Sackville, where he had planned to eat at the famous Marshlands Inn. Just before we reached the town A.B. stopped the car and said, "Do you like Coca Cola?" "No." "But this is Cape Breton Coca Cola; it's different." Whereupon he produced two bottles of the most powerful Coca Cola I had ever tasted.

Ten minutes later we entered the cosy foyer of the Marshlands Inn. Dr. George Trueman, who was the President of Mount Allison University, met us at the door. "The Lord has sent you," said he, "we have been having a conference of United Church ministers here all day and we are just going in to dinner. You both must come to the head table and say a few words to the brethren about your great work." The odour of that Coca Cola rose like incense around our heads as we made our way to the head table. However, it has been a familiar odour in the Maritimes for over two hundred years, and I think we made not too bad an impression. That same night in Moncton, A.B. had some three hundred co-operators holding on to their benches as with jokes, stories and solid economic precept he talked of the long history of exploitation in the Maritimes and the necessity for free men through joint planning and study to own and control their own economic resources.

"How can we get people to participate to a greater degree in the political processes of the country and bring some measure of realism into our own democracy? This can only be done," he pointed out, "by introducing democracy into business. Business of the people, by the people, for the people, will eventually place the ordinary citizen in a position where he will take a positive attitude towards his own and the nation's problems. That time will come," he said, "when the people have learned how to secure goods and services for themselves through co-operative action. There is only one safe road to economic change, not by violence and revolution, but through the long sure processes of education. I know of no safe depositories

of the ultimate powers of society but the people themselves, and the most effective medium that can be used
to this end is a programme of adult education in which
people come together to think and study and plan
their own destiny."

At midnight that meeting was over, and A.B. left
to drive through the night back home to be ready for
a similar meeting the next night at Reserve Mines,
Cape Breton.

This was the way these men of St. F.X. worked,
and as a result of their inspired and tireless efforts
the co-operative movement has become an integral
part of the social and economic life of the working
people of the Atlantic Provinces. So much so that at
the end of 1950 there were some 500 credit unions,
with 100,000 members and total savings of about
$10,000,000. There were consumers' co-operatives'
stores doing an annual business of about $40,000,000.
There were also wholesale co-operatives, co-operative insurance, co-operative housing, medical and
hospitalization services. A bi-monthly paper, *The
Maritime Co-operator,* which is the official organ of
the movement, has a circulation of 15,000. But the
intangible results of the Antigonish programme are
to many people even more important than the
improved living standards of people. These are
apparent mainly in the changed attitudes of thousands
of miners, fishermen and farmers. Most of the defeat-
ism that characterized their lives as a result of long
years of poverty and defeat has disappeared. There is

a new spirit of confidence and belief in the capacity of ordinary working people to think and plan and finally to achieve their own social and economic betterment.

Primary producers are adopting a more scientific approach to their occupation; there is a far greater interest in improved school facilities and higher standards of teaching; there is an enlightened interest in public health and less opposition to the necessary taxation to maintain such government services; religious intolerance has largely disappeared. Perhaps more important than anything else is the growing conviction that the people themselves can, if they wish, build a new and better social order and a more stable economic system.

14

The Farm Forum

A MAJOR PROBLEM of the CAAE in its early days was to find the best way in which to supplement the adult education activities of the universities, the Provincial departments of education and agriculture, and our affiliated voluntary organizations. The primary function of the Canadian Association for Adult Education as set forth in the charter was to serve as a clearing-house and co-ordinating agency. But it became apparent at once that we needed a national programme of our own if we were to become well enough known to command the attention and support of the public we were supposed to serve.

The answer to this need came indirectly through the Canadian Broadcasting Corporation and as a result of the close relationship we had maintained with that body since its establishment in 1936.

In the spring of 1938 I was asked to undertake a survey of school broadcasting in Canada. Gladstone

Murray, General Manager of the CBC, was under pressure at the time regarding the establishment of a department of school broadcasting within the framework of the CBC. He was therefore anxious to have a fairly complete report on the work already being done under the departments of education in the various Provinces. Since I would be in and out of all these departments during the coming year in the course of my regular duties it was thought that I could quite conveniently undertake the job. The CBC made a welcome contribution of $1,000 towards the costs of such a survey, and about a year later I turned over to the CBC a voluminous report not only on what was going on in school broadcasting in Canada but in Great Britain and the United States, together with certain recommendations concerning a school broadcasting department within the CBC.

In looking over reports on educational broadcasting in Great Britain I was impressed with the attempts (not very successful by the way) the British Broadcasting Corporation had made to establish a system of organized listening groups in the British Isles. It seemed to me that it might be worth while to attempt a similar experiment in Canada. In the British Isles the listening group had failed largely because it had to compete with a vast network of other well established community activities. The winter isolation of the Canadian farm family and the fact that the CBC was already proving a priceless boon in keeping farmers in daily touch with markets, the world of entertainment and events, might prove a vital factor in making the use of such a technique successful. Besides, the BBC listening group programme was not directed to any one group. It was a programme of general cultural interest; an organized listening group project which dealt entirely with the problems of rural life in Canada might succeed where the other had failed.

In the summer of 1939 Donald Buchanan, who was the Director of Talks for CBC, Gladstone Murray and I talked the matter over and decided that a first step would be to discuss the idea with the leaders of organized agriculture across Canada. We were convinced that if such a programme were to be successful it would have to deal specifically with the economic, social and educational problems of the people who made their living on the land. Preliminary discussions were held with H. H. Hannam, President of the recently formed Canadian Federation of Agriculture and others, and it was decided to arrange a series of radio interviews with the leaders of the farm organizations in the Provinces throughout Canada. Since a major interest among farm people was the development of the producers and consumers co-operative movement, the interviews would deal in the main with co-operatives and credit unions as media for the improvement of general living standards in rural areas. Neil Morrison, who was doing post-graduate work at McGill, was suggested as one who was well equipped to conduct such a programme.

I have always been interested in what might be called "the hotel room interpretation of Canadian Enterprise." In almost every undertaking in which I have been involved, preliminary plans have been worked out with a small group of interested people in a hotel room somewhere in Canada. This was inevitable in my case, because for the first ten years of my term as Director of the CAAE a large part of my life was spent in hotels from Charlottetown, P.E.I., to Vancouver, B.C. Very often my only opportunity to discuss our plans with Provincial colleagues was to invite them to spend an evening with me in my hotel room. I suspect that the same is true of a great many national organizations in Canada. It was perhaps natural, therefore, that the preliminary steps leading up to the establishment of the National Farm Radio Forum should have taken place in a hotel room.

Arrangements were made for a meeting in the Chateau Laurier in Ottawa between Gladstone Murray, Donald Buchanan, Neil Morrison and myself at 10 a.m. one morning in the summer of 1939. This was a meeting Neil missed, and thereby almost changed the shape of his destiny. He had missed the morning train from Windsor Station in Montreal, had hired a taxi to take him to the Montreal northend station where he caught a train which got him into Ottawa about 3 p.m. Unfortunately he had spent all his money on taxi fare and had no money to buy himself a meal on the train. He came straight to the CBC building, to which we had adjourned after lunch, and

for the next two hours we discussed our plans. At the
end of that time he pathetically informed us that he
had had no food all day, and what's more had no
money either to get a meal or get back to Montreal.
This situation was soon remedied, but when we
realized how sharp he had been during the afternoon
while starving for food we arranged to pay him a
monthly salary which was bound to keep him hungry
for the next six months. Jointly the CBC and the
CAAE agreed to pay him $100 a month and expenses.
That series of broadcasts started in British Columbia
in October and was scheduled to continue once a week
throughout the winter until the series would end
in the Maritimes with Dr. M. M. Coady and A. B.
MacDonald of Antigonish as panel members.

The broadcasts, which dealt in the main with the
extent and values of the Co-operative Movement,
were extremely well received by farm people generally,
and by co-operators in particular, but they awakened
a certain amount of resentment among the champions
of free enterprise. One morning when I reached my
office I found a copy of a letter sent to me by a friend
in Western Canada, which emanated from some group
of people in the west. and had been distributed to all
the members of Western Boards of Trade. The letter
pointed out that these radio interviews were "inimical
to private enterprise," and urged the brethren to get
in touch with their local members of Parliament and
insist that the series be terminated. By that time Neil
Morrison had interviewed leading members of farm

organizations in Western Canada, had reached Montreal and was booked there for two broadcasts, one with the English-speaking leaders of the co-op movement in the Eastern townships and one with their French-speaking colleagues. I had been listening whenever possible to the radio interviews, and managed to catch the first one from Montreal. After the broadcast was over the announcer said, "This brings this series of broadcasts to an end." I almost went through the roof. There were four more broadcasts to come, and they had been widely advertised. Besides, everyone was looking forward to the story of the St. Francis Xavier Co-operative Movement and its dramatic successes among the fishermen, farmers and miners of the Maritimes.

The following day I telephoned Gladstone Murray and he informed me that there had been objections to the programme and it was thought wise to examine these complaints before proceeding further with the talks. This seemed to me to be a straight case of political interference with the CBC so I angrily informed Mr. Murray that unless the programme was continued as scheduled I would have to release the story to the press. When I received no reply from Gladstone Murray the next day, I called up Judith Robinson who was at that time the brilliant and militant columnist of the *Globe and Mail*. She came up to the office and I showed her a copy of the circular I had received, and told her that while I had no proof, I felt certain that this was a flagrant example of government interference with the CBC. At that time the late George McCullough, publisher of the *Globe and Mail* was at war with the CBC and was looking for a stick to beat it with. I don't believe this in itself would have had any special significance for Judith Robinson; she is a woman of integrity and was indignant at the idea of farm people being deprived of their rights as Canadian citizens. She wrote a blazing column dealing with the incident next day and the same evening the *Telegram*, which certainly had no love for the CBC, attacked the government for what appeared to be interference with a public utility which belonged to all the people.

To make a long story short the broadcasts were continued and the programme proceeded as scheduled. Not long ago I met Gladstone Murray in the University Club in Toronto and reminded him of the episode. Then I said, "Why didn't you telephone back when I told you I would give the story to the newspaper?" His answer was one I fully understand. "Don't you see," he said, "I wanted the story to get to the newspapers; that was the quickest and most effective way to put an end to that sort of meddling."

At the end of that winter's experience, Neil Morrison joined R. Alex Sim, Director of the Macdonald College Rural Education Service in a programme called "Community Clinic." This was a series of twelve broadcasts presented regionally in Quebec by the CBC in co-operation with Macdonald College. Together these two young men organized groups of listeners among the English-speaking farm people of Quebec; prepared the broadcasts and took part in them; sent out mimeographed study bulletins with questions attached; and groups were urged to send in reports and comments on the content and quality of the broadcasts.

It should also be noted that as early as 1937 an experiment which had a definite bearing on the development of Farm Forum was tried out in Bruce and Huron counties, Ontario, by Harvey MacDougall, educational secretary of the United Farmers of Ontario, in co-operation with a local radio station. This experiment had shown that a discussion group programme organized around a radio broadcast was a technique that promised great possibilities. Also a major factor in the events leading up to the organization of the National Farm Radio Forum was a series of pamphlets entitled *Canadian Farm Problems* prepared by Dr. W. H. Brittain of Macdonald College. The sixteen pamphlets in the series were designed to make available to rural study groups sufficient factual and reference material, with suggested questions to enable them to discuss any particular economic problem in a critical manner. The series of booklets were prepared in such a way as to make them admirably suited for study group purposes. At the beginning of its history these pamphlets gave the new organization a solid backlog of scientific information and stimulating material to work on.

By the fall of 1940 plans had advanced to the stage

where it was decided to try out a Farm Radio Forum programme on an eastern network, under the joint sponsorship of the CBC, the CFA and the CAAE. Neil Morrison had by this time joined the newly-formed Farm Broadcast Department of the CBC under Orville Shugg, who was then supervisor. This department in co-operation with the Canadian Federation of Agriculture and the CAAE has been responsible for the National Farm Radio broadcasts ever since.

The people who deserve a major share of the credit for developing the techniques which had made the NFRF one of the most effective radio educational programmes anywhere are Orville Shugg, Neil Morrison, H. H. Hannam, R. Alex Sim, Dr. W. H. Brittain, Leonard Harman, Ruth MacKenzie and Ralph Staples. There were many others, of course, but these people were at the directing end of the experiment at the beginning and gave the programme its content and momentum.

When war broke out in the fall of 1939 the government early in October accepted the offers of four national voluntary organizations to supply the troops with educational and welfare services: the YMCA, the Canadian Legion, the Knights of Columbus and the Salvation Army. The Minister of National Defence immediately established a Directorate of Auxiliary Services with the President of the Dominion Command of the Canadian Legion as Director. Under this administration the general activities of the four national agencies were defined, and it was announced that all civilian agencies working with the troops would come under the jurisdiction and supervision of District Officers Commanding, assisted by Deputy Directors of Auxiliary Services. From henceforth auxiliary services would be a military establishment under the Adjutant-General, formed with the objective of unifying all such services for land, air and naval forces.

While all of the auxiliary services provided educational and recreational facilities, the Canadian Legion was assigned the major responsibility for formal and informal education. Colonel Wilfrid Bovey, then Director of Extension for McGill University, was that year President of the CAAE and Chairman of the Canadian Legion Educational Committee and as an organization we were invited to co-operate in every way possible in carrying out this assignment. The Director and a great many of the leaders in adult education throughout Canada became immediately involved in the Legion's educational programme —Robert England and Andrew Moore of Winnipeg, Dr. John Robbins and Dr. H. M. Tory of Ottawa, Guy Henson and H. B. Chandler of the Maritimes, Ross Winter of Queen's University, Dr. W. J. Dunlop, Dr. Floyd Maine of the University of Western Ontario, Dr. Gordon Shrum of U.B.C., and many others. But the Association had no direct responsibility in the field, and the job to which we were committed went steadily forward.

In 1941-1942 Farm Forum went on the national network, and has continued as a weekly programme for farm people ever since. It has fairly consistently served an organized listening audience of some 30,000 people in groups of from ten to twenty who report weekly on their findings and on general group activities. The programme has achieved world-wide recognition and its techniques have been adapted for the same purpose in several other countries, notably India and the British West Indies. In 1954 UNESCO published a 255-page book called *Canada's Farm Radio Forum,* which was the product of a two-year survey of the project. It will be used as a guide to other countries contemplating the use of a similar kind of programme.

Over a period of fifteen years the National Farm Radio Forum has made a great contribution to national unity in that it has brought together once a year or more the leaders of agriculture from every part of Canada, and through its weekly broadcasts has provided a common basis of understanding between the farm people of western and eastern Canada. Within the communities involved it has created a new sense of neighbourhood and hence of social responsibility. It has provided a medium through which farm people by studying, talking and planning together have arrived at a sharper understanding of local and national problems. It has strengthened farm organizations by creating a greater sense of the dignity and human values in farming as an occupation. Through action projects (which are the lifeblood of any organization) the Forums in hundreds of Canadian districts have discovered that by working together in tolerance and good-will it is possible to revitalize the social and economic life of a community with higher standards of public health, improved methods of agriculture and a new sense of community responsibility.

As an experiment in adult education it has proven its value and will continue, even though changing demands may change its form and emphasis.

IN OCTOBER, 1939, I was in the office of Dr. Frederick P. Keppel, President of the Carnegie Corporation of New York, when I received a long distance telephone call from the Honourable Mr. Euler, who was then Minister of Trade and Commerce in the Canadian Cabinet. He was speaking from Ottawa and he asked me if I could attend a meeting in his office at 10 a.m. the following Monday. This was on a Saturday, so I went directly from New York to Ottawa and presented myself as requested at the Minister's office. There were assembled one or two Cabinet Ministers and Deputy Ministers, among them the Honourable Mr. Crerar; one or two non-governmental people, among whom I recognized my friend Dr. Walter Murray, President of the University of Saskatchewan, who had, I think, just retired that year.

John Grierson had been in Canada in 1938 and

had drawn up the plans for the National Film Board. I had met him on several occasions, and, like everyone else, was impressed with his intellectual brilliance and his vast knowledge of and experience in the production of documentary films. There was a lengthy discussion of the terms of reference of the proposed new National Film Board, and before the session adjourned for luncheon, I was asked if I would accept an appointment as Director of the Board. I had lunch with Dr. Walter Murray, who urged me to accept the offer. I explained that I was only in my third year as Director of the Canadian Association for Adult Education and that it would be, in my opinion, unfair to the organization to abandon it in its infancy. At the afternoon session I pointed out that Mr. Grierson was somewhere in California at the moment and that he had forgotten more about film production than I could possibly learn in five years or more, and I urged Mr. Euler and his Associates to find out his whereabouts and offer Mr. Grierson the job of Director. After some discussion it was decided to follow my advice.

It is a matter of history that Mr. Grierson accepted and the National Film Board of Canada owes its reputation as one of the finest institutions of its kind in the world to his genius and inexhaustible energy.

I am proud to have had some small part in this.

15

Various Experiments and Projects

MEANWHILE the Association had become involved in two projects of a clinical character, one in northern Manitoba and the other in Simcoe County, Ontario. It had long been my conviction that research work in adult education could best be carried out at the community level. People who were active in this field in Canada were for the most part so deeply involved in the active promotion of different types of programmes that little attempt had been made to assess their value in terms of community betterment and citizenship responsibility.

It happened that Rev. Harry Avison, who was then a United Church minister in a Manitoba rural community, and Miss Esther Thompson, head of the Women's Institutes in Manitoba, had for some time been discussing the possibility of a citizenship training centre to be conducted somewhat after the fashion of a Scandinavian Folk School. But the problem was, how to finance such an experiment and where it should be established. The Winton family of Minneapolis had large timber holdings in northern Manitoba and operated a mill employing some 500 men at The Pas. Dave Winton, the President and General Manager of the company, was a friend of Miss Thompson, and during the course of a conversation she discussed with him the idea of trying out an adult education experiment somewhere in Manitoba. Dave Winton immediately suggested that The Pas would be an ideal place for such an undertaking.

The Pas was a town, at that time, of about 3,000 population, situated at the point where the Hudson Bay Railway on its way to Churchill crosses the Saskatchewan River. It is almost 500 miles from Winnipeg and the same distance from Churchill. At the time of which we are speaking its mixed population made it almost a microcosm of Canada racially. There were roughly 1,200 of British stock, 700 French, 500 Ukrainian, 200 Polish, 200 Scandinavian, 150 German. There was as well the large Cree Indian reserve across the river from the town. It had good schools and churches, a music festival, a little theatre, Board of Trade, Women's Institute, and an active business and professional life. There were all the accompanying religious, political and social organizations that are found where varied cultures meet.

The largest single industry was lumbering with approximately 500 men employed in the mill in summer and an equal number in the logging camps in the winter. In addition to the problems created by its mixed population there was the comparative isolation. The nearest large town and settled community was an overnight train journey away, and in those days there were only three trains a week. It seemed to be a community ideally suited for the kind of experiment we had in mind. Experience had shown that very often a well organized adult education programme designed to serve the interest of the whole community could unite its citizens (of all races) in a way that nothing else could do. Already the Dominion Youth Training project, which was set up by the Federal Government in 1936, had been operating in hundreds of western communities with great success, and reports showed that in addition to its values in training young men and women in occupational crafts it was having a marked effect in uniting the young people of the district in a common undertaking.

Mr. Winton was definitely interested in Esther Thompson's proposal and in November, 1937, he invited Harry Avison, his wife Mary and myself to spend a week-end in Minneapolis to talk over the plan. The outcome was that the Winton family agreed to put up money enough to cover the costs of a three-year experiment, sponsored by the CAAE with Harry Avison in charge. In January, 1938, the

Avison family moved to The Pas and the work got under way. The Youth Training courses directed from the Manitoba Department of Labour were available as a starting point, and with their co-operation thirty young men and women representing eleven nationalities were given six-week courses in such home problems as food, clothing, home nursing, child care and citizenship. Two instructors were sent in to give the main courses. Mary Avison conducted the courses in child care and Harry in citizenship. Soon study groups in public affairs, local community programmes and English classes for new Canadians were organized. Fourteen young Ukrainians and Slovaks took the classes and Harry, who was teaching the class, was put on the spot one day when a bright-eyed young Slovak girl asked: "Why is it that in my country we are poor, we have nothing, but everybody is happy; and in your country you have money and cars and everything, and nobody is happy."

When I visited The Pas in September, 1938, the programme had broadened out to include: (a) recreation—crafts, folk dancing and singing, (b) playground supervision, (c) film showings in the lumber camps in winter, and (d) a youth council representing all nationalities. A reading room and pamphlet information service had been in operation for some time, and in every way the experiment seemed to be flourishing. The Avison's house was full of young people every night and Harry and

Mary Avison were guide, counsellor and friends to large numbers of young people of all races. Nevertheless, I came away with the feeling that the inherent difficulties in the situation would eventually defeat any two people, however able and patient they might be. I doubt if we could have found anywhere in Canada any two persons more dedicated than the Avison's; wise, patient and flexible enough to get on with any reasonable group of citizens.

But the community itself was disjointed and amorphous. There did not appear to be any solid core of backing for the work the Avisons were trying to do. It seemed to me that there was an unbridgeable chasm of suspicion between the foreign groups and those of English-Canadian origin. But the major difficulty was the fact that David Winton was unwilling to allow the family name to be connected with the undertaking, the reason being, I think, that he feared that the project might be regarded by the more radical elements among his workers as a kind of sedative to keep them quiet. Thus the question kept coming up—Who is financing this effort? It was not the Provincial department of education. It was not the University of Manitoba. The Youth Training Commission of the Federal Government helped with the technical training courses, but that was all. Then it was explained that the Canadian Association for Adult Education was paying the shot. The people had never heard of it—it must be a communist set-up.

It was rumoured that the Avisons spent a lot of time with the foreigners. One woman, who was prominent in the Women's Institute, invited me to tea while I was in The Pas, in order to let me know "what was going on." The Avison children went to school in overalls—"girls mind you." Mr. Avison didn't go to church regularly. At a meeting at which he presided they sang *Oh Canada* instead of *God Save the King*. She had been told on good authority that Mrs. Avison was a Jewess. And so on *ad nauseam*. It takes a long time to outline and eventually defeat that kind of underground attack. We had only three years to complete the demonstration. It was not long enough, and the CAAE was not at that time well enough known to give the experiment the authority it needed.

At the end of the three-year period, and the coming of World War II, the project was discontinued, and Harry Avison and his family moved to St. Anne de Bellevue, where he had accepted a position as Professor of English at Macdonald College. While the programme at The Pas was getting under way, I was working every spare moment when not at the head office at a dozen other things. Among them the Community Life Training Institute, with headquarters in Barrie, Simcoe County, Ontario. For this project we were able to obtain a grant from the Carnegie Corporation and further assistance was provided by W. J. Dunlop, then director of the Department of Extension, University of Toronto.

This experiment under the direction of David Smith was, over a period of ten years, one of the most successful the Association has ever sponsored. In a happy co-operation between local school boards, agricultural societies, the church organizations and recreational directors, rural summer schools in recreation for children, short courses in agriculture, the teaching and training of leaders in discussion group techniques, film councils, etc., were arranged in almost every district in Simcoe County.

It was during the busy summer of 1937 that I received a call from Sir Edward Beatty's secretary asking me to meet him in his suite at the Royal York Hotel. For many years Sir Edward had been one of the chief supporters of Major Fred Ney and his National Council of Education, and as chairman of the Board of Governors of McGill University he was an important figure in higher education as well.

On the occasion of my visit with him in September, 1937, he explained that he was anxious to set up within the framework of the CPR an informal educational system which would make it possible for any young CPR employee anywhere in Canada, whether he was an office worker, section hand, mechanic or brakeman, to have within easy reach the opportunity to study and train for advancement. A committee had already been appointed with J. C. Bonar (at that time council member of the CAAE) as secretary and J. Murray Gibbon as chairman. I suggested to Sir Edward that it would be necessary to have a full time director of the project. He agreed and asked me to recommend someone. I immediately mentioned the name of Fred Stone, who was then secretary to Mr. Aberhart, Premier of Alberta, and shortly afterward Sir Edward interviewed Stone and offered him the job.

Fred Stone is now head of the CPR Department of Research; but for three years from 1937 till the spring of 1940 he directed an adult education programme within the framework of the CPR which provided lecture courses in a wide variety of subjects for thousands of CPR employees throughout Canada. The most spectacular part of the project was the establishment of the Canadian Pacific Foundation Library. By the end of the first year of the experiment 16,000 sets of books, each set containing ten books on economics, history, public speaking, English, etc., had been distributed to CPR employees. In 1940 the exigencies of the war changed the emphasis in their programme, but much of the work initiated in those years has continued.

In the summer of 1938 the annual meeting of the Canadian Educational Association took place in Halifax, N.S., and Dr. Henry Munro, who was then Deputy Minister of Education for Nova Scotia, was by fortunate circumstance the President both of the CEA and of the CAAE. He had somehow persuaded the Board of Directors of the CEA to allow a fairly large place on the programme for consideration of adult education and its claims upon the provincial educational authorities for encouragement and support. In order to strengthen our position with the representatives of provincial and municipal governments whose representatives made up the governing body of the CEA Dr. Munro as President of CAAE had invited Dr. Albert Mansbridge, founder of the Workers Educational Association in Great Britain, to come over as a special speaker for the occasion. Another guest was Dr. Morse A. Cartwright, who had been one of the founders and was then Director of the American Association for Adult Education.

A further departure from the regular procedure of the CEA was that arrangements had been made to make the occasion a moving feast with meetings in Halifax, N.S., Saint John, N.B., and Charlottetown, P.E.I. At the first day's sessions in Halifax, papers were given by Morse Cartwright and myself dealing with the general purposes and some of the achievements and working philosophy of adult education. That evening a mass meeting was held in Convocation Hall at Dalhousie University, where Dr. Mansbridge was the main speaker. Mansbridge had a thick Lancashire accent, almost as pronounced and colloquial as that of Stanley Holloway. He was a stout man with an extremely humorous appearance and habit of speech. He explained at the outset that it didn't much matter what subject was announced for him, it would turn out to be "the saaame speech he had been maaakin' for nigh on forty years an all." There was a lot of meat in what he had to say but he had the audience so convulsed with laughter most of the time that it was more like a vaudeville performance than a serious discussion. Unfortunately, what he told us in Halifax was in fact true, for at similar meetings in Saint John and Charlottetown he made speeches under different headings but in substance much the same. By the time the Charlottetown meetings were over the staid and serious representatives of formal education in Canada had had about all they could take of adult education.

After the conference sessions at Saint John, we were driven by automobile to Cape Tormentine, where the ferry takes off for Prince Edward Island. On the way, the conference delegates were entertained at a special convocation in Mount Allison University, Sackville, where Morse Cartwright and I were given honorary degrees.

An incident occurred at Charlottetown that almost finished me as director of the newly-formed CAAE. It happened that plans had been made for a panel discussion on adult education to take place before the assembled delegates at 8 p.m. in the ball room of the Charlottetown hotel. Among the participants were to be Morse Cartwright, Dr. Munro and myself with John Croteau as chairman. There was a free afternoon for sight-seeing that day, and Bram Chandler bundled Morse Cartwright and his wife, Croteau, Dr. John Robbins and myself into his library truck and took us forty miles up the Island on a trout-fishing expedition. We found the roads

a bit difficult and it was three in the afternoon
when we arrived at the mill-pond. There were two
leaky old boats with homemade oars available, and
Croteau started off in one with Morse Cartwright
and his wife, while Chandler, Robbins and I took
the other. Even with the two Cartwrights on the
stern seat Croteau outweighed his passengers, and
as they started off up the lake he appeared to be
rowing down the side of a mountain. We fished till
about 6 p.m. and by that time we had taken four
dozen trout averaging from 10 to 12 inches long.
So we called it a day, had lunch on the shore and started
homeward. But what with bad roads and car trouble it
was nearly nine o'clock when we got back to Charlottetown. The panel discussion was over and the delegates to the conference took a dark view of some
of the people, especially myself, who were supposed
to take a leading part in the conference.

In the summer of 1942 I was invited to assist in
a project which had been initiated and financed by
the Rockefeller Foundation under the Foundation's
programme in the humanities. This was a socio-
logical study of the semi-arid plains of the northern
United States and the southern areas of Manitoba,
Saskatchewan and Alberta. The ultimate purpose of
the survey was to arrive at a description of the
region, an enumeration of its basic problems and their
likely solution. By this means it was hoped that the
people of these areas might eventually come to a

better understanding of their situation and of ways of improving it. A conference of rural economists and agricultural leaders was called to meet in Nebraska in June, 1942, and Mr. Watson Thomson, who was then Director of Extension at the University of Manitoba, was asked to head up a small group of experts to prepare in study outline form the findings of the survey which had been proceeding for more than a year.

Mr. Thomson enlisted the following persons to assist in preparing the report of the survey and the study outlines based upon its recommendations: Dr. Carl F. Kraenzel, Rural Sociologist at Montana State College, Dr. Glen H. Craig, Agricultural Economist at the same institution, and myself.

During the months of August and September the three of us settled down in the Bozeman Hotel and turned out a manuscript of 200 mimeographed pages called *The Northern Plains in a World of Change.* There were four parts in the study. Part I dealt with World Issues and the Plains Farmer; Part II, The Uniqueness of the Plains; Part III, Plains Agriculture at the Crossroads; Part IV, Challenge to the Plainsman. Each part was divided into chapters outlining the history of the region; the region and the community; patterns of ownership and control; problems of credit, technology, marketing, social institutions, etc.

A meeting of experts was called by the Rockefeller Foundation to review the manuscript, suggest changes and generally prepare the work for publication. This meeting was held in the Bessborough Hotel, Saskatoon, during the first week in October, 1942, and was attended by twenty people representing the universities and departments of agriculture of Alberta, Saskatchewan and Manitoba, North and South Dakota, Montana, Wyoming and Nebraska. There were also representatives of the three western wheat pools; editors of farm journals; H. H. Hannam of the Canadian Federation of Agriculture; and David H. Stevens and John Marshall of the Rockefeller Foundation.

I presided at this editorial conference, and four days and nights were spent in a page by page examination of the manuscript. With a good many changes it was finally approved for publication. The book was published by the Rockfeller Foundation in two formats: one in which each chapter was issued separately as a study pamphlet with a series of questions for discussion, the other in hard-cover book form. It was distributed for use in Canada by the Canadian Association for Adult Education and in the United States by an organization called The Northern Great Plains Advisory Council. I understand the book was widely distributed and studied by Adult Education groups in the Western States, particularly in the region covered by the survey, but it received only slight recognition in Western Canada.

Nevertheless, it was an interesting experience, and it might be worth the while of some post-graduate student in rural sociology or economics to examine the document now, sixteen years later, to discover how much, if any, of its forecast and recommendations have been justified by time.

16

Citizens' Forum

AT A CAAE CONFERENCE held in Macdonald College during the week between Christmas and New Years, 1942, a good deal of discussion centred around the possibility of a national radio programme after the fashion of the Farm Radio Forum, but directed to people in Canadian towns and cities who might be interested in regular study and discussion of national and international problems.

Already the CBC had led the way for such an experiment through a series of panel broadcasts called "Of Things to Come," chaired by Morley Callaghan and produced by Rupert Lucas. These weekly programmes originated in Canadian cities, using local authorities as panelists, and the subjects covered a wide range of domestic and international interests. Study bulletins were not sent out, but

166

the discussions were later published by the CBC and widely distributed. It was suggested that arrangements might be made with CBC to continue the series under the title "Of Things to Come — A Citizens' Forum" with the CAAE undertaking to organize listening groups and provide study outlines. The idea was enthusiastically endorsed at the annual meeting held in London, Ontario, in May, 1943, and it was agreed that a general conference should be called to meet at Macdonald College, St. Anne de Bellevue, in September, for the purpose of promoting general interest in the project.

We were all aware that it would require a good deal of extra money to carry out our part of the work. George Grant had been added to our staff in February, 1943, and he and Jean Morrison, wife of Neil Morrison, began at once to prepare study outlines and make plans for the September conference. During the summer of 1943 I was constantly on the lookout for additional funds, without any very great success. Once I found myself on the train from Winnipeg to Toronto with the late Edgar Tarr, who was then national chairman of the Canadian Institute of International Affairs, and I suggested that his organization should become joint sponsors of the programme with the CAAE. He was very encouraging and promised to discuss the matter with his Board of Directors. My plan was that both organizations should contribute $5,000 to the cost of promotion and publications. The CBC, I felt, might contribute a like amount, and the names of the sponsoring organizations would appear on all publications and be mentioned on the broadcasts. Mr. J. M. Macdonnell, M.P., who was then a prominent member of the Board of the CIIA, was enthusiastic about the idea and gave it his whole-hearted support. But it was felt by some members of the CIIA that it would be a radical departure from tradition and the terms of reference of the organization to promote or share in public debate of controversial questions, and thus the plan for joint sponsorship with CIIA fell through.

Meanwhile plans for the Macdonald College Conference were proceeding and I was in despair about being able to finance the whole project. But the Canadian Council on Education for Citizenship came to the rescue and at a meeting of its Executive held at Macdonald College on June 19, 1943, voted $1,000 to meet the costs of calling and organizing the September Conference. Harry Avison was appointed organizing secretary and plans immediately got under way.

The theme chosen for the September Conference was "Education for Reconstruction," and within a few weeks discussion leaders and speakers had been chosen. The main addresses were to be given by Dr. Howard Y. McClusky of the University of Michigan, Dr. Walter Kotschnig, Professor of Education at Smith College, and a member of the U.S. Commission to study the organization of peace, Dr.

J. S. Thomson, General Manager of the Canadian Broadcasting Corporation, Squadron Leader Gregory Vlastos, Professor of Philosophy at Queen's University, and others.

Invitations were sent out to hundreds of organizations and individuals, and on the opening day 135 delegates, representing every Province in the Dominion, registered for the two-day conference. Three commissions were set up to work out in detail the plans for the broadcasts.

(1) The Commission on Methods was chaired by the late Dr. David Petegorsky, then of the War Information Board in Ottawa. This Commission dealt in detail with problems of promotion of the programme by use of films, publications, the co-operation of affiliated bodies, etc.

(2) The Commission on Organization, chaired by Donald Cameron, Director of Extension at the University of Alberta, outlined the organization of the whole project at three levels—national, provincial and community.

(3) The Commission on Curriculum was chaired by Neil Morrison of the CBC. In this Commission 60 people examined the outlines of study material previously prepared by George Grant and Jean Morrison, and suggested new titles.

At the final meeting of the conference the reports of the three Commissions were unanimously adopted. Morley Callaghan was invited to become permanent chairman of the weekly broadcasts. Provincial committees were appointed to promote the undertaking and to organize listening groups, and it appeared that "Citizens' Forum" was away to a good start. But there was trouble ahead.

The first National Committee for Citizens' Forum was made up of representatives of a number of organizations, all of which were engaged in public education of one kind or another. The CBC was represented by Neil Morrison, Morley Callaghan and Marjorie McEnaney; the Canadian Institute of International Affairs by Dr. Malcolm Wallace and Douglas MacLennan; the YWCA by Jean Hall; the YMCA by Murray Ross; libraries by Richard E. Crouch of London, Ontario; the WEA by Sydney Robinson; Canadian Congress of Labour by Dr. Eugene Forsey; the Navy and Army by Lieut. C. D. C. Graham, for the Director of Naval Education and Major Z. Phimister for the Director of Army Education; for the CAAE, E. A. Corbett (chairman), George Grant (secretary), Jean Hunter Morrison and Leonard Harman. This committee was later enlarged to include representatives of business and industry through the representation on the Advisory Board of members of the Canadian Chamber of Commerce and the Canadian Manufacturers' Association.

It was as representatives of this Committee that Neil Morrison and Morley Callaghan proceeded to Ottawa to consult with government officials and others regarding a choice of speakers for the seasons' panel broadcasts. They had made out a partial list of participants, but violent exception was taken by two prominent liberal members to several of the speakers from the opposition parties whose names were on the list. The feeling in the matter became so violent that one member of the Mackenzie King Cabinet announced that the CBC would not be permitted to proceed with the programme. This story quickly got to the press, and it was immediately pounced upon by some newspapers as an example of government interference with the CBC.

I was in Winnipeg at the time during the course of a western trip, and I had been urging our western Provincial committees to prepare for the coming broadcasts by organizing listening groups and ordering supplies of the bulletins accompanying each of the subjects to be discussed. Neil Morrison called me by telephone and informed me of the crisis, and the next morning I went to the *Winnipeg Free Press* and discussed the matter with the editors, G. V. Ferguson and Dr. J. W. Dafoe. I remember that Dr. Dafoe ran his fingers through his tousled hair and then said, "Edward, my boy, this makes my trigger finger itch." He called Grant Dexter, then the *Free Press* representative in Ottawa, asked him to get the details of the story and call him back. The next day there was an article in the *Free Press* attacking the King government for interference with the CBC, and shortly afterward Dr. A. Frigon,

General Manager of the CBC, gave a statement to the press in which he declared that the programme would go on as originally planned. Thus for the second time we were successful, thanks to the press, in defeating an attempt to restrict the freedom of the CBC.

The Citizens' Forum in the thirteen years of existence has commanded a listening audience of approximately half a million people. It has never had as many organized listening groups reporting regularly as the National Farm Radio Forum has had. The latter has averaged over the years about 1,000 groups of from 10 to 20 people, whereas the Citizens' Forum average would be more like 200 to 300. It is likely, however, that Citizens' Forum has enjoyed a larger individual listening audience, and now that it is on both television and radio it undoubtedly has a very much larger body of followers than ever before.

Most Canadians who have followed the programme since its beginning are agreed that it has been a stimulating and extremely valuable experience and that the project has done much to clarify public thinking on important questions.

In the matter of promoting national interest in Citizens' Forum, credit must be given to the services of the universities, departments of education and many voluntary agencies throughout Canada which granted the project their encouragement and support from the beginning. Members of our executive in the various provinces also did a great deal to stimulate interest: Professor Gordon Shrum of the University of British Columbia, Donald Cameron of the University of Alberta, Professor Kenneth Gordon of the University of Saskatchewan, Watson Thomson of the University of Manitoba, Dr. Floyd Maine of the University of Western Ontario, Professor C. H. Stearn of MacMaster, W. J. Dunlop of the University of Toronto, Professor Harry Avison of McGill, Guy Henson and Charles Topshee of Nova Scotia, and many others. But in an undertaking of this kind, staff work is perhaps more important than any other factor, and I cannot close this chapter without paying tribute to the headquarters staff of the CAAE for their devotion and loyalty during these trying years, when salaries were small and financial insecurity was an ever-present nightmare. The work of George P. Grant (now head of the Department of Philosophy at Dalhousie University), who joined our staff in 1943, and of Jean Hunter Morrison, editor of our magazine, *Food for Thought*, deserves special praise. These two carried a major part of the load in preparing the study pamphlets and in promoting interest in Citizens' Forum and in all of the activities of the Association. Later in 1945 and 1946, Martin Estall (now Professor of Philosophy at Queen's University) and Robert Mac-Kenzie, who has since achieved an international reputation as an author and commentator on the BBC, joined our staff and gave notable service during the year or more they were with us. But all of these would agree that the addition of Isabelle Wilson to our working force in 1945 gave new strength and intellectual content not only to Citizens' Forum but to every interest and activity of the Association.

17

Frenzied Finance

THE MOST difficult job in connection with the establishment of a national organization of a purely voluntary character is the business of getting money enough to keep it going during the early years when it is unknown and before it has been accepted by the public as an important and useful association.

This is particularly true if the society has to do with education. By its very nature adult education must deal with controversial questions. The discussion group is the chief cornerstone of any worthwhile programme of public education, and our history shows that this is the stone the builders often reject. Our Farm Forum programme and later our Citizens' Forum were at the beginning suspected by large numbers of people. As was often said to me, "You never settle anything, you are just getting people stirred up. Leave these questions to be settled by the men who through their training and experience know the proper answers." One prominent Toronto business man invited me to lunch one day and proceeded to belabour me and the association because we had published in connection with our Citizens' Forum programme a pamphlet written by one of Canada's most distinguished economists to which he took violent exception. In many quarters the Association was regarded as "left wing," a term used by many people to describe any organization or individual whose opinions differ from their own. The fact of the matter is that the association in its various programmes has been scrupulously careful to present all sides of any question it discusses, and has always been non-partisan in its policies.

In the first years of the Association history, money was hard to come by. As has already been stated, we had annual support from the departments of education in British Columbia, Saskatchewan, Ontario, Nova Scotia, New Brunswick and Prince Edward Island. We also had from 1936 to 1944 an annual grant of from $7,000 to $10,000 a year from the Carnegie Corporation.

A direct appeal for the support of almost any kind of welfare work had a good chance of success anywhere in Canada, but at the beginning of our work it was exceedingly difficult to make a case for adult education. There is nothing very exciting to the average business man in the reports of study group activities, leadership training courses, library services, etc. You can point out to him that a well-informed community interested in solving its own problems is usually a happy and contented one, and that domestic processes are not likely to flourish where ignorance and prejudice prevail; but I have found that the prospective donor is much more likely to be generous if he has faith in the kind of people whose names appear as directors of the enterprise and those who have already shown their interest by contributing fairly large amounts of money. The fact that the Carnegie Corporation of New York had continued to make an annual grant, that the departments of education and the universities supported the movement, and that men like Dr. Henry Munro, Deputy Minister of Education for Nova Scotia, Sir Robert Falconer, W. J. Dunlop, Dr. W. L. Grant, of Toronto, Colonel Wilfrid Bovey of McGill had been among the founders of the CAAE, that Dr. Sidney Smith, President of the University of Manitoba (now President of the University of Toronto) was for three years President of the Association gave it an appearance of stability and respectability that stood us in good stead most of the time. But finding the money for an operation of this kind was never easy, and it is still difficult.

In 1944 when I returned from Great Britain I found that the Carnegie Corporation had decided to discontinue its annual grant to the Association. This was a shock, but not unexpected, since it has always been the Corporation's policy to make their grants available for periods of three and five years, and they had now been contributing to our work for eight years. That fall the situation looked desperate indeed. We had started the Citizens' Forum the year before and had taken on three additional staff members. Unless I could find another twenty thousand dollars we would have to cut both staff and programme.

In November, Dr. Sidney Smith, Principal of University College at that time and also President of the CAAE, and Roland Michener, M.P., who was Chairman of our Finance Committee, called a meeting of a few business men in the University Club to acquaint them with the work of the Association and to consider plans for raising money. As a result of that meeting and some follow-up work by Roly Michener and myself, about five thousand dollars was contributed. It was a start, but not nearly enough. Shortly after that I went to Montreal and managed to get an appointment with John W. McConnell. I had known Mr. McConnell slightly during my undergraduate days, and as a matter of fact got my first introduction to the business of fund raising under his inspiring direction. In 1915 he was chairman of a very large group of Montreal business men who were responsible for raising money in that area for war relief. At that time I was secretary of Strathcona Hall at McGill University, and I was asked to canvass a list of professors and students on McGill campus. It was the custom to meet for lunch every day during the campaign, when reports of the amounts collected by the various team captains were handed in. Mr. McConnell, an extremely handsome and debonair figure, presided at these luncheons, and called out the names of the captains in turn. One would hold up cheques to the amount perhaps of $25,000—loud cheers. Another might report $30,000—louder cheers. I always sat at the end of the table and reported my returns last, usually anywhere from $50 to $100. The contrast was always good for a laugh, but it was good-natured laughter and I was never humiliated.

However, one day Mr. McConnell took me to one side and said, "I have a card here I would like you to take. It bears the name of Mr. —— who lives on Pine Avenue. He is an extremely wealthy man, retired now, and none of our canvassers has been able to get inside the door. He used to be an elder in Erskine Presbyterian Church. I understand that Dr. Andrew Mowatt, late minister of Erskine Church, was an uncle of yours. Perhaps you could use that connection to get in to see him. The committee feels that he would contribute at least $5,000. See what you can do."

The next day I telephoned the house, gave my name and explained to Mr. ——'s secretary or butler, whichever it was, that I was a working member of Erskine Church, a nephew of the late Dr. Andrew Mowatt, and that I would like to see Mr. —— about a very important matter. After quite a delay the voice on the telephone said, "Mr. ———— would like to know if you are a son of the Reverend Thomas Corbett." I said I was. "Well, Mr. ———— knew your father when he was a student at Pine Hill College in Halifax and he would be very happy to see you at 10 a.m. tomorrow morning."

Next morning as I made my way up to Pine Avenue my head was full of visions of the sensation I would create at the day's luncheon when instead of reporting a miserable $20 or $30 I would wave in the air a cheque for five thousand dollars. The house was one of those old-time palatial residences on Pine Avenue, facing the mountain but with windows at the back looking over the city with the St. Lawrence in the distance. I was admitted by an aged butler and shown into the library where I waited for perhaps fifteen minutes. Presently a door opened at the back of the room and Mr. and Mrs. ———— entered. They were very old but carried themselves very erectly and with great dignity. They welcomed me warmly and immediately began to talk about the good old days in Nova Scotia; they got out old magazines with photographs of Dalhousie students, and spent a good deal of time finding a picture of my father. We went around looking at old books, some rare paintings, and finally the fine old people asked me if I would like to see the bed in which King Edward slept when as Prince of Wales he visited Montreal. It was 11.30 before I finally got a chance to explain the purpose of my visit. I gave them the card and a list of names with the amounts already given, and stated that Mr. McConnell felt that $5,000 would be an appropriate contribution. Mr. and Mrs. ———— retired to an office just off the library, and presently returned with a sealed envelope. I thanked them and explained that I had to hurry away to report at the daily luncheon.

Mr. McConnell presided and there were the usual jubilant reports from the team captains. When my turn came I explained what a friendly reception I had had, and how the morning had been spent reminiscing about Nova Scotia; then I walked up to the head of the table and presented my envelope to Mr. McConnell. He opened it, looked at the cheque, and burst into laughter. Then he stood up and waved the cheque in the air. It was for $100.00.

Now in the fall of 1944 I was to meet Mr. McConnell again. I had no hope that after thirty years he would even recall my name, and as I waited in his office I was a little nervous and uncertain about my reception. In these thirty years Mr. McConnell had become one of the wealthiest and most powerful men in Canada. He is also one of the most generous. When he strode into the room, he was as slim and handsome as he was when I had last seen him. Apart from the fact that his hair was now white there was scarcely any change in his appearance. As he shook hands, he was laughing heartily and his first remark was, "Do you remember the time I sent you to canvass Mr. ———— on Pine Avenue?"

I mention all this because in half an hour Mr. McConnell had not only gone straight to the heart of the problem but had given me the soundest possible advice about the best way to present my case in asking large corporations for assistance. He began by saying that of course he would help, but he said, "I think it would be most unwise to ask for large contributions. "You say, you need $20,000. It would be far better to have 20 gifts of $1,000 each than four of $5,000; then if one of your donors dropped out it would not be such a serious matter." With Mr. McConnell's help I soon had pledged fifteen annual contributions of $1,000 each and the balance of the twenty thousand in smaller amounts.

Six years later when James Muir, President of the Royal Bank, became President of the CAAE he greatly expanded the area of interest in our programme and the number of business and financial institutions contributing to our support. Also under Mr. Muir's direction a sound pension scheme for the staff of the Association was set up, and the beginnings of a reserve fund established.

I suspect my method of raising funds was never orthodox and perhaps not very subtle, but it was in most instances effective. Mr. McConnell had told me always to try to see the President or General Manager of the company or financial institution I intended to ask for support. This I was almost always able to do. It was my custom to write a personal letter to the chief executive of the organization, asking for an appointment. If I was fortunate enough to be granted an interview I sent in advance a dossier of information about the Association. Almost without exception I found that when I was finally admitted there was a copy of our correspondence on the desk of my host, and his first few questions revealed the fact that he had taken time out from a very busy life to get a clear understanding of what we were trying to do. But after a few minutes we discovered that we had other things in common, and from that moment the conversation might wander off in any direction. It always seemed to me a good idea to avoid a quick decision, and I could usually anticipate a refusal before it was actually made. In such circumstances I led the conversation off in some other path, either a good story or reminiscences about familiar territory. I don't mean that a man with the experience and sensitivity of the chief executive of a big organization is fooled by such a technique, but the fact is that very often a grant of money is made on a personal basis of liking and friendship. This I had found to be true also in dealing with the big Foundations, granted always, of course, that the appeal had merit in itself.

The time allotted for these interviews was in most instances half an hour, sometimes less, but they nearly always went far beyond that, because we usually found that we had acquaintances in common or were both familiar with people and situations in various parts of Canada. The late George Spinney,

President of the Bank of Montreal, soon discovered that we were both born and brought up in Nova Scotia, and we talked for nearly an hour about conditions in the Maritimes and fishing in Digby Harbour. At the end of that time he called his secretary and asked him to make out a cheque for $1,000.

When I first met Mr. James Muir, President of the Royal Bank, we spent a hilarious half-hour swapping yarns about Cape Breton and Scotland, and I remember Mr. Muir stated at one of our meetings during his second year as President of the CAAE that "that man Corbett had beguiled him into accepting a second term by telling him stories about Cape Breton."

Mr. Charles Dunning, President of Ogilvie Flour Mills and Chancellor of Queen's University, told me of his early life as a homesteader in Saskatchewan, and I recall that he said, "You don't have to convince me of the value of adult education, it's the only kind I've ever had."

The late Mr. Gordon Leitch, President of Toronto Elevators, one of the most gracious and generous of men, discovered that as President of the Canadian Handicrafts Guild I knew a good deal about Canadian craftsmen and the quality of their work. This was a hobby of his, and during the year he contributed to our organization we had many long talks on the subject.

With the late Richard Law, President at that time of the United Grain Growers, I spent a delightful evening in his suite in the Royal Alexandra Hotel in Winnipeg. Most of the time we spent in reminiscences of his early days as a farmer in Southern Alberta. A few days later he sent me a cheque for $2,500 as a grant from his company.

Frank B. Common, Q.C., a colleague of mine at McGill and one of my cherished friends, was a great help to me in obtaining the kind of personal introduction to the heads of large business firms which made it possible to meet in an atmosphere of friendliness and goodwill.

I remember my appointment with the late J. S. McLean, President of Canada Packers. I had written him asking for an appointment and shortly afterwards his secretary telephoned and asked me to have lunch with Mr. McLean at the Toronto Club. During the meal he never once mentioned our organization, but when it was time to go he said, "I know about your work, in fact, I was once on one of your Farm Forum panels, remember? Agnes McPhail was on the same panel and of course she had always taken a dark view of me. During the discussion I expressed my understanding of and complete sympathy with the plight of the Canadian farmer; whereupon Agnes leaned into the microphone and shouted, 'Well, blow me down!' How much money do you want?"

I have mentioned here only a few of the men and corporations among our early supporters. With one or two exceptions the first twenty have continued to be among our good friends and have continued their support. There are many more contributing now, but I would like at this point to say that in the past twenty years I have interviewed a great many "big business men" both in Eastern and Western Canada and in every instance except one I have found them courteous, friendly and anxious to help. I was not always successful, of course, but it is worth noting that the only occasions when I was summarily dealt with (with the one exception noted above) was when I was trying to negotiate with someone other than the President or General Manager of the firm.

Since those early years the work of the CAAE has become much more widely known, and now enjoys the confidence and support of provincial and federal government departments, organized labour and agriculture, universities, and some eighty Canadian business corporations.

18

The Wartime Information Board

EARLY IN 1942 T. W. L. MacDermot and I were asked by Herbert Lash, director of the Wartime Information Board, to come to Ottawa for the purpose of organizing a Dominion Speakers' Bureau, with branches in each of the Provinces. The purpose of the plan was to make available to voluntary agencies throughout Canada a list of speakers who would be ready to address meetings of citizens in connection with the various war efforts — Victory Loans, plans for postwar rehabilitation, etc. The Provincial Committees were to be organized in each instance under the chairmanship of the Lieutenant-Governor of the Province.

Terry, who was then Principal of Upper Canada College, obtained leave of absence from his post and gave all his time to the work, while I agreed to spend at least two days a week in Ottawa as his assistant.

During January, 1942, we journeyed together through the West to the Pacific Coast, leaving behind us formidable committees headed by the Lieutenant-Governors of Manitoba, Saskatchewan, Alberta and British Columbia. Then in February we succeeded in setting up similar working units in the Maritime Provinces.

Perhaps the most interesting and colourful of all the people we met and talked with on those trips was Archie McNab, Lieutenant-Governor of Saskatchewan. He entertained us at Government House and far into one night we listened with delight to his talks of the early West. He asked us immediately for our first names and then said, "Call me Archie." To him we were Ned and Terry from then on. One of his stories concerned the stay of the late King George and Queen Elizabeth at Government House in 1939. Apparently his homespun charm had the same effect upon their Majesties as upon everyone, for before they left it was "George" and "Archie" between himself and the King. This story he climaxed with another equally impressive. His son was one of the most famous of Canadian pilots in the early days of World War II, and when he came up before the King at Buckingham Palace to receive his second decoration, King George said to him, "Why didn't you tell me the first time you were here that you are a son of Archie McNab."

Some of the Provincial Committees were active and useful until the end of the war; others existed in name only and were completely inactive. On the whole, however, the effort seems to have been worthwhile.

I mention this period of service with WIB at this point mainly because it leads up to another episode in the history of the CAAE which is perhaps worth recording. I think it was in June, 1942, that I reported for duty at the WIB offices in the new Supreme Court Building, only to find that the administration had been changed almost overnight and the eviction of the staff had been carried out with such dramatic suddenness that Herb Lash, the Director, had already gone, and Walter Herbert, Assistant to the Director, was seated at his desk in the hall outside his office with his files around him, getting ready to leave the government service.

Later that same day I was asked to attend a small meeting in the Department of External Affairs. The meeting was called by Tommy Stone, now Ambassador to the Netherlands, then one of the top men in the Department of External Affairs in Ottawa. I was invited, I presume, as Director of the CAAE. The purpose of the meeting was to discuss the best possible use to be made of a gift of $50,000 from an unnamed donor in England who was anxious that something should be done for the young men from Britain who were taking their Air Force training in Canada.

After some discussion it was agreed that the job was of sufficient importance to require the full-time services of a Secretary or Director. I immediately thought of Walter Herbert, who was temporarily unemployed as of that day. Someone telephoned and asked him to come over, and within an hour Walter had started a new career, and one which has been of increasing importance to Canada ever since that day. Until the war ended the fund was used to equip the various camps throughout Canada, where young RAF personnel were stationed, with silk-screen reproductions of Canadian paintings and books and magazines dealing with Canadian history and current events. Arrangements were made with nearby universities for lecture courses and guided tours of historic sites, records of Canadian folk-songs were provided, and every effort made to enable the young men to become acquainted with Canadian history and Canadian life.

When the war ended the value of this kind of effort to inform people from other lands about Canada and its people so impressed the members of the committee in charge that the Canada Foundation was immediately established with Walter Herbert as Director, a position he still holds. The Canada Foundation and the Canadian Association for Adult Education have worked closely together since 1945 to the benefit, I believe, of both organizations.

My short experience as a part-time employee of the Wartime Information Board also led to one of the most interesting experiences of my lifetime. In 1944 the WIB began the publication of a series of

pamphlets called *Canadian Affairs* under the editor-
ship of Squadron Leader Gregory Vlastos, then on
leave from his post as Professor of Philosophy at
Queen's University. In the foreword to Volume I,
No. 1 of the series the *raison d'être* of the experiment is stated as follows:

The force that is smashing Hitler and Hirohito
today is not a military machine, but a military team.
And the team is defeating the machine. In a military
machine all the thinking is done at the top. It is the
privilege of those who drive the machine. In a military team thinking must be done at every level. It
is the duty of every last member of the team. That
is why *Canadian Affairs* exists today. Men who think
need tools with which to think.

In 1941 the British War Office had set up the
Army Bureau of Current Affairs. Ever since, the
ABCA bulletins, *War and Current Affairs* and *The
British Way and Purpose,* had formed the basis of
weekly talks and discussions carried on in training
hours, and were considered just as much a part of a
soldier's training as instruction in automatic weapons.

General A. G. L. MacNaughton put the same
scheme into force in the Canadian Army and asked
for a Canadian publication to supplement the ABCA
bulletins, to keep the Canadian troops in touch with
the life and problems of their own country. The
answer to his request was the overseas edition of
Canadian Affairs. In Canada too, the Army put
ABCA into the training programme. The Navy and

Air Force also made the study of current events a part of initial training. In addition to all this, hundreds of informal discussion groups were getting started in all three services. The articles were straightforward and factual, designed to help the student think for himself, and each pamphlet carried questions for discussion.

It is of interest to look back years afterwards and observe some of the titles of the fifty-two pamphlets issued:

> *War-changed Canada*
> *The New North*
> *Canada—World Trader*
> *People on the Land*
> *Price Controls for Victory*
> *Power for Prosperity*
> *Will There Be Jobs?*
> *So You Want to Be a Farmer, etc. etc.*

The second pamphlet, Vol. I, No. 2, called *Future for Fighters* was written by myself. It was a detailed listing with some comment of the provisions of the new rehabilitation scheme, at that time just an order-in-council.

Partly as a result of that effort I was asked by WIB to go overseas to visit Canadian troop centres throughout the British Isles for the purpose of meeting the men in the various army camps to tell them about the provisions already made for their return to civilian life. Robert Westwater, then Inspector of Public Schools in Ottawa who had been

active in the Canadian Legion Educational Programme since its inception, was to accompany me
and perform the same service for the RCAF. We
were to fly to Halifax the first week in May, 1944,
and from there we were booked on the *Empress of
Scotland* to Liverpool.

Before we left, David Dunton, Director of WIB,
arranged a briefing session with the Ottawa heads of
the armed forces. This was a memorable experience.
Mr. Dunton presided, and Westwater and I sat properly humble and somewhat over-powered at the foot
of a long table lined on each side with the top brass
of the Army, Air Force and Navy. After a good deal
of talk about the manner in which our mission was
to be carried out, one elderly officer of high rank
spoke up. He did not believe that it was a good
thing for the morale of men soon to go into action
to be thinking about what was going to happen to
them after they got out of the Army. The war had
still to be won and it was no time to be talking
about civilian rehabilitation. "I suggest," he said,
"that these two gentlemen, if the Wartime Information Board thinks it useful, go to England and talk
to the troops about some of the pleasant things
going on at home in Canada—hockey, baseball, war
production on the land and in the factories, show
some films, tell them stories, etc., but keep off this
business of rehabilitation; it's bad for morale."

There was a murmur of applause from one or
two other officers, and then David Dunton turned to

Bob Westwater and myself and asked us if we had any comment. As I remember it we both answered in the same vein—if the Wartime Information Board felt that the purpose of our mission was to entertain and amuse the troops, they had chosen the wrong people. Even if we were qualified to talk about hockey, and lead sing-songs, which we weren't, neither of us would be prepared to ask for leave from important jobs for such an enterprise. We had both served in World War I and we knew from experience that nothing boosts morale in any army abroad more than to be informed that the people at home are planning for their return to civilian life.

The Wartime Information Board had done its duty, it had consulted the top brass, now Mr. Dunton adjourned the meeting and we retired to his offices where all the details of our departure were worked out. The trip across the Atlantic was tiresome but exciting. There were four of us packed in a small cabin — Robert Westwater, myself, the late Major Bobby Bourne and J. A. M. Cook, war correspondent of the *Winnipeg Free Press*. Bobby Bourne was of course in uniform; we other three were the only civilians on the ship. There were some 5,000 air force and army personnel and more nurses than I have ever seen in one place before. There must have been 500 of them on board. After we left Halifax we were warned to sleep with our clothes on because of the danger of submarine attack. There were several warnings but a few days later we arrived safely in Liverpool.

In London we were met at Euston Station by Wing Commander Ross Winter, who was Director of Educational Services (Overseas) for the RCAF. The next day I called on Major General P. J. Montague, Chief of Staff of the Canadian Army, while Robert Westwater called on Air Marshal L. W. Breadner. Somewhat to my surprise I was not only warmly received by General Montague but I found that he was completely in sympathy with our undertaking. He was convinced that while the troops were anxiously waiting for D-Day, officers and men would welcome an opportunity to hear about the Rehabilitation Act and have an opportunity to discuss it. When I left GHQ General Montague wished me luck and asked me to come and see him again, as he would like to hear what kind of a reception I had been having.

Arrangements for my itinerary were in the hands of Lieut.-Colonel John Grace and Lieut.-Colonel Orville Ault, heads of educational services for the Canadian Army. I found that plans had already been made for me to spend two weeks or more in the north of Scotland with the Canadian Forestry Corps. There were about 6,000 Canadians in the Forestry Corps, scattered in units of 200 men, all the way from Beuly north of Inverness to Blair Athol.

The second week in May I proceeded to Edinburgh and arrived at the North British Hotel on a Saturday morning. Guy Henson who was with the Canadian Legion Educational Services and stationed in London, travelled with me on his way to a short course for army personnel being given at the University of Aberdeen. On Sunday, which was a wet, cold day, I suggested to Guy that since we were in the ancient citadel of Presbyterianism we should go to church at St. Giles Cathedral. It was so cold inside the church that we sat with our trench coats on throughout the service. The service of the Established Church of Scotland is highly ritualistic and to my amazement the lessons were read by two pallid youths with marked Oxford accents. "Ay will araise and go to my Fathah" sort of thing. As a son of the manse this annoyed me greatly and when the sermon was preached by a visiting clergyman with a thick Lancashire accent, I turned to Guy and whispered, "Shades of Jenny Geddes, what's happened to Scotland?" Now I am never very adroit at finding the right page in a book of responsive readings, and as usual I fumbled badly. There was a little old Scottish lady sitting to my left, and she reached over, took the book from my hand and in a loud whisper said, "Can ye no find the place?" She flipped over several pages, handed the book back to me and said, "There it is." The next time we stood up, I fumbled again, once more she took the book saying, "It's quite simple, ye know, if ye'd just pay attention." Then after the benediction we stood at attention to sing "God Save the King." I mumbled the words under my breath, and I could see out of the corner of my eye that the little lady was casting side glances at me. When we were leaving our pew, I turned to her and said, "Thank you very much for helping me." She looked me straight in the eye and said in a loud voice, "Ahve verra little use for a mahn that doesna sing God Save the King." I went out of St. Giles as happy as a youngster. Jenny Geddes was in her heaven and all was well with Scotland.

19

A Tough Assignment

BEFORE I left London for the north of Scotland, word of my arrival in England had somehow reached an old friend of mine, Dr. W. W. Hepburn, Director of Education for Ayrshire. He had been in Canada several years before when he had completed a survey of elementary and secondary education for the Province of Quebec, and later had spent a week at the University of Alberta looking over our extension programme.

There was to be a meeting of all the Directors of Education for Scotland at the Trossachs Hotel in the lake country near Glasgow, the last week in May, and I was cordially invited to attend and take part in the programme. Accordingly before proceeding to Inverness I took a bus from Edinburgh to the Trossachs Hotel. The Education Act of 1944 had been passed in the British House of Commons not long before and its provisions formed one of the major subjects for discussion. But the first item on the programme of the opening day of the conference was listed as an address by Sir Hector Hetherington, Principal of Glasgow University, on the vexed subject of "The Responsibility of the University to Society" or words to that effect. I gathered afterward that the Directors of Education had a feeling that Scottish Universities were too remote from the everyday problems of the people, and that there was too wide a gap between themselves as the men in charge of elementary and secondary education and the university.

This gap had been made more significant as a result of the section of the new Act which raised the school leaving age to sixteen and further demanded that provision be made for the continued education of young people leaving school up to the age of eighteen. In his address Sir Hector took the classical position that the function of a university was research and teaching and the maintenance of high standards of scholarship. That was its responsibility to society and if the Directors insisted upon the same high standards in their work there would be no yawning chasm between where their work ended and the job of the university began.

This annoyed Mr. Coutts Morrison, Director of Education for Stirlingshire, and from the back of the room he spoke somewhat as follows: "When ah notissed your subject, Sir Hector, ah wonderred what ye'd have to say. Ah've listened to ye for three quarr-

ters of an hour and ah've only one comment to make
and that is that Plato two thousand years ago haad
a far better understanding of the true meaning of
education than you have." From then on the discussion was frank and extremely outspoken, but everyone enjoyed it mightily, including Sir Hector, who
joined in the laughter which followed Coutts Morrison's comment as heartily as everyone. The whole
conference was a delight. The thrust and parry of
the argument, sharpened by wit and by Scottish
humour, was something for a Canadian to see and
hear. It made our educational conferences seem tame
by comparison. The last evening of the meeting the
Directors, by way of a jolly farewell to myself, joined
hands around me, sang Auld Lang Syne and, signing
off for the night, taught me what Coutts Morrison
declared was the Scottish Educator's national anthem:

The de'il took a walk round the fit o'Ben Lomond
　　An skinned his behind on a muckle big stane

An auld wife was takin' a walk in the gloamin'
　　An she took him doon tae her hoose at the fit o'
　　Dunblane

She fed him and clad him, and in her bed laid him
　　But the darty auld deevil would no sleep alane

If anyone wants the next two verses he'll have to
write to me or see Donald Gordon, President of the
CNR. I'm told it's one of his favourite songs.

　　A day or two later I reported for duty at the
Forestry Corps headquarters which was situated on

the estate of Lord Lovat, the famous founder of the Commandos. From this vantage point the whole Forestry Corps programme was directed and here my itinerary was worked out. I was taken in charge by a Major Maxwell who was director of education for that branch of the service. The Corps headquarters was overcrowded and the Major said he would telephone to the Drum-na-Drochit Hotel (about ten miles away) for a room. Hotels in Scotland at that time closed at 11 p.m. and he promised the manager he would have me over there before closing time. That night about 200 officers and other ranks crowded into a dimly-lit mess hall, and I gave my first overseas exposition of the terms laid down in the rehabilitation scheme. I spoke for about twenty minutes, during which time I made a quick run-down of the provisions of the Act and then threw the meeting open for questions. Interest was so keen and there were so many questions that it was almost eleven o'clock before the meeting adjourned. At that time of year in the north of Scotland darkness only lasts a few hours and although it was 11.30 when we reached the Drum-na-Drochit Hotel it was still broad daylight. But the hotel was closed. We tried the front door and the back door, but there was no answer. We were just about to turn away when a man appeared at an upper window and a stern Scots voice shouted, "Ye promised to be here at eleven o'clock; ah think it's well, when ye make a proomis,

tae keep it; ye'll no get in here tonight." Bang went
the window and we made our way back to the Corps
headquarters where I squeezed in beside Major Maxwell for the night. The next day I was admitted to
the Hotel and a charming, comfortable place it turned
out to be.

The next two weeks I covered all the Forestry
Corps Camps, speaking often morning, afternoon and
evening. The question periods were exciting and
often difficult. In one camp a tough-looking lumber-
jack proceeded to make a speech from the floor. He
began by saying, "I'm a communist and I don't care
who knows it." Then he launched into a hysterical
harangue. The rehabilitation plan, he said, was just
a bone thrown to a dog to keep him quiet. After the
war soldiers would be selling shoelaces just as they
did after World War I, etc., etc. At this point the
officer presiding said to me, "Shall I slap him down?"
I said, "If you do, I'll lose this meeting. A lot of
these lads think he's right." When my turn came to
answer I told the ancient story of the conversation
between Lenin and St. Peter at Heaven's Gate.
Everyone laughed, including the commie, and we
went on happily with the question period without
further interruption.

I think on the whole this was the toughest assignment I ever had. The physical drag and nervous
strain of three periods of questioning a day, all of
which lasted at least an hour was terribly exhausting,
but it was at the same time one of the most reward-

ing experiences of a lifetime. At the end of two weeks we had finished the job and Major Maxwell and I headed south to Edinburgh.

On our way south the highway skirted the famous Culloden battlefield and we stopped to have a look at it. Major Maxwell had been there before and as he led me around the historic field he pointed out the landmarks. Here was an enormous stone in the centre of the field and cut into the rock was the inscription, "Here stood Prince Charlie." Another stone not far away carried the inscription, "Here stood the MacIntosh," and so on around the field, but down by a small spring was a tiny moss-covered stone on which were the scornful words, "The Campbells, they're buried here."

I arrived in London the day after D-Day, and a week later in a Canadian Army camp in Surrey I saw my first buzzbomb. I had about 200 men around me in an open field near the parade ground, and we were deep in a discussion about rehabilitation plans, when the thing passed over our heads at a height of about 500 feet. It cut out a quarter of a mile away and exploded. From then on I felt that Hitler had my number because they followed me everywhere. I was having lunch in the Regent Palace when a buzz-bomb tore one side off the hotel. I moved out to Walton-on-Thames, but they were worse out there than in London. When my work took me to Sussex camps they were coming in there. It was all very exciting.

It was not easy to keep all the appointments made for me and to get there in time. Once I left Exeter, where I had been helping with a short course for army education personnel, on an early morning train, and was to be picked up at a wayside station not far from London and driven to a Canadian army camp near Seaford in Sussex. The train was late, my driver was late in picking me up, and when I arrived about 3 p.m. a company of some two hundred officers and other ranks had been waiting on me under some trees in dripping rain for a half hour. I know from experience in the First War how maddening an experience of that kind can be, and as I got out of the jeep and walked toward my audience I knew very well they were fed up with visiting civilian lecturers. There were curses, not loud but ominous, in the atmosphere. After a young Brigadier introduced me I began by asking, "Are there any Nova Scotians in the crowd?" About 50 hands went up. So I said, "O.K., you chaps will remember the name of James Gillis, the famous Cape Breton poet. One time he wrote an Ode to Queen Victoria and the first verse went like this:

> Here's to thee, Queen Victoria,
> In all your bright regalia,
> With one foot in Canada
> And the other in Australia."[1]

[1] I have found out since from W. A. Deacon, author of *The Four James's* and literary editor of *The Globe and Mail*, that this poem was written by James Gay, not James Gillis.

Well, I've been living for the last month with one foot in Scotland and the other in the South of England, and it's impossible to be everywhere on time. Anyway I'm sorry I'm late." From then on we had a good time together in spite of the rain. This was the occasion when a squat little Cape Breton sergeant stood up right behind the commanding officer and said, "I'm a miner from Sydney, Cape Breton, and I'm suspicious of every g-d-d-n thing that comes out of Ottawa. My father was in the First World War for five years and all he got out of it was a kick in the arse." At this point a voice at the back shouted, "Sit down Scottie yer rockin' the boat." Then there was a chorus, "Sit down and shut your trap." Later I said to the Brigadier, "This is a citizens' army all right. These men don't hesitate to speak their minds even in front of their officers." "Of course," he said, "that sergeant is one of the best men we've got. He's entitled to his opinion."

On my second visit to Edinburgh late in July of that summer, my son Bruce, who was a bomber pilot in the RCAF, joined me for three days on leave before taking off with his crew for Burma. It was a happy occasion for both of us. We spent our time visiting historic sites, saw a few shows, played a little golf, and lived in great luxury at the North British Hotel where the bathtub in our room was so big that one used a small step-ladder to get into it. At the end of his three days leave I saw Bruce off on the train to London and proceeded to Aberdeen, where

I was to assist in a short course for Canadian service men and women arranged by the Canadian Legion Educational Services. While in Aberdeen I stayed at the Imperial Hotel, and one morning at breakfast a young Naval officer sat down opposite me and said, "Hallo, Uncle Ned, how are you." It was my nephew John Corbett of Edmonton, whose ship was in port for a few days. He had seen my name in the hotel register the night before and had come in to have breakfast with me. This was my first contact with the Canadian Navy, and that night I had dinner with John's fellow officers and a very jolly occasion it proved to be.

Meanwhile I was very anxious to get back home to my work. I had left the CAAE in a precarious position financially and it had not improved during my absence. Transportation back to Canada was difficult to get, but through the good offices of the Honourable Mr. Massey, who was then Canadian High Commissioner in London, a place was found for me on a Lancaster bomber, and in the company of a half-dozen RCAF officers I flew back to Canada in August. On November 11th word came to us that Bruce and his crew were missing in Burma. That was a difficult time for all of us. Paul was an officer with the Canadian Army somewhere on the Western front. Joan was in hospital with a detached retina in her right eye. The telephone became a terrifying instrument during the next two months. We were

always hoping for some word of Bruce, and we were
of course anxious about Paul and Joan. It was early
in January, 1945, that we finally learned that Bruce
had been shot down near the Chindwin River in
Burma and he and his crew of five had been found
dead beside their plane on November 8th. I have
never been able to understand why it took so long
to learn the truth about Bruce and his crew. Since
all supplies to the British Army in Burma were provided by airlift, communications between headquarters and the battle front must have been daily and
hourly. The wreckage of the plane was found the
day after it was shot down. The bodies were buried
in the jungle the following day, but we were not
notified until two months later. But it was good to
look back to those three days we had had in Edinburgh. One show we saw was headlined by the late
Will Fyfe, and one of the stories he told in his inimi-
table Scottish dialect I shall never forget. An aging
Scotsman began to think about his latter end and
decided to get some estimates on the cost of a
funeral. There were two undertakers in the town,
one very expensive and one who performed his services at a much lower cost. One day the old man
went downtown determined to get a final price from
each of them. He first visited Mr. McTavish, who
operated the more expensive of the two establish-
ments, and the conversation went something like
this:

"Mr. McTavish, what do ye charge for a guid

funeral? Ahm no deed yet, but what would ye charge tae pit me doon in the ground?"

"Weel, Angus, ah can gie ye the best hearse and the black horses wi' the big plumes on their heads. I can gie ye a guid oak coafin wi' brass handles and a copper plaque on the top o' it. Ye could have twa keeners — old widdow MacInnis and her sister — the Reverend Dr. Chalmers to read the service, and the whole thing would cost ye 30 pounds, ten shillin's and sixpence.

"Och," said Angus, "yon's an awfy lot o' money jist tae pit a man in a hole in the ground, ah'll just rin along ap the street and see auld Johnny Maclean, yer opposition." At the Maclean establishment the same bargaining went on. Finally Maclean said:

"Ah've got just as guid a hairse as McTavish, and ah've got black horses wi' the same kind o' plumes on their heeds; now wits the sense o' an oak coafin. I can gie ye one made of birch and ye'll never know the deefrance. It'el hae brass handles and a copper plate and the whole thin'll cost ye 20 pounds, ten shillin's."

Well, this was a saving of ten pounds so he went back again to see McTavish for further bargaining. But old McTavish would have none of it.

"Rin awa' Angus and get Maclean tae pit ye doon, but ah'll tell ye this, yon birch coafin, it'll be jist like yin o' thae cheap suits o' clothes ye get at the service stores in Glasgow; yer behind will be out of it inside of three weeks."

20

The Joint Planning Commission

ACCORDING to its charter, the major function of
the Canadian Association for Adult Education is to
serve as a clearing house for adult education in
Canada. There are other purposes outlined in the
charter; to develop interest by means of publications,
radio and conferences; to provide for study and
research in methods; to undertake experiments and
demonstrations. But from the beginning this function of co-ordination was considered to be of primary
importance. It was never intended that the organization should attempt to standardize adult education
or to direct it from a national office. Programmes
were to be worked out locally in co-operation with
existing organizations, and directed by people on the
spot who were familiar with local needs. The function of the new association was to offer advice based

on a thorough knowledge of theory and proven practice.

It was not thought of by the founding fathers as necessarily a programming organization; but an organization cannot operate in a vacuum. It was first necessary to become known and accepted. Such activities as the national Farm Radio Forum, the Citizens' Forum, our magazine and other publications, our work with universities and departments of education, voluntary organizations and individuals, gradually made the name of the association known throughout the country.

Nevertheless it was not until 1945 and the end of the war that we were in a position to set up a standing committee to implement the first and perhaps most important function of the CAAE.

The events leading up to the establishment of the Joint Planning Commission are important steps in the history of the association and need to be recorded here. The war had brought new challenges and responsibilities. Our close association with the Canadian Legion Educational Services had made us aware of the crying need, not only in the services but among civilians, for readable information on subjects related to the war and the confused issues of the times.

As far back as 1940 we began sending out mimeographed bulletins on wartime questions of public interest. The material for these pamphlets was prepared for us by the Canadian Institute of International Affairs and retailed at ten cents a copy. It may be of interest at this time to look at some of the titles we were distributing. There were:

> *French Canada and the War*
> *War Aims and Peace Plans*
> *India and the War*
> *United States Neutrality*

These must have been exceedingly well done, because I recently found in my files the following editorial from the *Winnipeg Free Press* of December 5, 1940:

There is nothing slow about the Canadian Association for Adult Education these days! Even in times of peace it consistently kept in touch with large masses of people and guided and directed and sustained their search for knowledge and insight: and now that Canada has become engaged in war the Association is redoubling its effort to be of service.

Its latest enterprise is aimed to meet a widespread demand which has arisen throughout the Dominion for literature dealing with problems in connection with the war. And in conjunction with the Canadian Institute of International Affairs (which supplied the material) it is issuing from its headquarters at 198 College Street, Toronto, a series of bulletins of informal character.

And those to hand, one dealing with French Canada and the War and the other with War Aims and Peace Plans, commend themselves by their meaty, factual content and their lucid presentation. The general reader who wants to be informed on these aspects of Canadian war problems will be amply repaid for his modest outlay of ten cents per pamphlet. He will have material that is not immediately available in other accessible form, and he will have it in language that delineates the usual obscurities with striking clarity.

Later we collaborated with the Canadian Institute of International Affairs in the production of the Behind the Headline series. Also in 1940 in co-operation with The Ryerson Press we started a rather ambitious book publishing business with the high-sounding title of the New Dominion Books. Six of these were published[1] before we discovered we had entered a highly competitive field and decided to stick to the bulletin and pamphlet type of informational service.

In 1940, largely through the efforts of the Honourable C. H. Blakeney, who was then Minister of Education for New Brunswick, the Canadian Council on Education for Citizenship was organized, and for the next five years or more the two organizations (CAAE and CCEC) built up a network of communications through which the information materials of the Wartime Information Board, the National Film Board and the Canadian Broadcasting Corporation were distributed to thousands of schools and adult education groups.

[1] *The Conduct of a Meeting* by W. G. Frisby.
Five Political Creeds by members of the staff of Queen's University.
Child Psychology for Parents by Prof. B. A. Fletcher.
The Cornerstone of Democracy by Prof. John MacDonald.
An Epistle to the Hebrews by John Cournos and Dr. C. E. Silcox.
How to Arrange a Public Dinner by W. G. Frisby.

It was largely as a result of this experiment in co-operation that the Joint Planning Commission came into existence.

In June, 1945, the annual meeting of the CAAE was held in Winnipeg, and it was at this conference that the original draft of a programme planning commission was brought forward and formally adopted. It was the product of many minds and a great deal of preliminary discussion. I remember sitting in John Grierson's room in the Fort Garry Hotel till almost dawn with Harry Avison, John Robbins, Neil Morrison, Geoff Andrew, George Grant and others, discussing the probable values of such a commission, while Grierson, to my amazement and envy, demolished a huge bowl of caviar and chopped onions.

The primary purpose of the new commission, it was agreed, was to provide a medium through which the valuable collaboration which had been developed during the war years could be continued. It was only in this way that we could avoid overlapping in programme planning, publications and the production and use of films. Money was needed to get the plan in operation, and once again the CCEC (now the Canadian Citizenship Council) came to the rescue and carried the costs of the first meetings of the commission. Later, in 1947, the Carnegie Corporation provided a grant for a small secretariat. The first meeting was held in Ottawa in the fall of 1945 and was attended by representatives of some twenty organizations. It has grown until it now has a membership of about 100. It is an oddly assorted group. There are film and radio producers, Federal and Provincial government department representatives, university extension directors, representatives of the Chamber of Commerce, the Congress of Labour, the Canadian Federation of Agriculture, research departments of the banks, the National Y's, the Teachers Federation, the Canadian Jewish Congress, Church organizations, and so on.

The Joint Planning Commission has an odd organizational set up. On the one hand it is a standing committee of the CAAE. This provides it with secretarial services, an office and a small budget. But at the same time it is a loosely knit combination of many organizations that have no allegiance to or organic tie with the Canadian Association for Adult Education.

The Commission meets three times a year successively in Ottawa, Montreal and Toronto.

It has performed a most valuable service in that it has made a friendly family of the organizations and the people who are at work in the field of education. By establishing awards in radio, films and in adult educational projects it is progressively improving and maintaining standards of quality in the work being done. The Henry Marshall Tory Award for distinguished service in adult education; the Canadian Film Awards; and the Canadian Radio Awards, have already been recognized as important national activities in these fields. The Joint Planning Commission has in the past twelve years largely fulfilled a major purpose of the Canadian Association for Adult Education. The services of Walter Herbert, Director of the Canada Foundation, and of Mrs. W. H. (Clare) Clarke, as chairman and secretary respectively, have been in large measure responsible for the continued success of the undertaking.

21

What I Believe

MY CAREER as director of the Canadian Association for Adult Education came to an end in the spring of 1951. I had been fifteen years on the job and was full of dreams about spending the rest of my life fishing, golfing and "makin' the round of my garden."

The staff of the organization and the members of the Executive felt that the occasion called for some form of celebration—not to say rejoicing—and a farewell party was held in the Arts and Letters Club, Toronto. There were something like 200 people present and the dinner and the meeting which followed were presided over by Dr. Sidney Smith, President of the University of Toronto. It was one of the happiest and at the same time most moving experiences of my lifetime. Kind things were said; a large sheaf of telegrams (unsolicited, of course) were read; and I

216

was presented with a television set—the gift of friends in every part of Canada. But I think all were agreed that the highlight of the meeting came when Mary Ferguson read the tribute written by her husband, George V. Ferguson, editor of *The Montreal Star,* which my friend Mr. L. W. Brockington, Q.C., has insisted on including in his generous introduction to this book.

In Conrad's *Lord Jim,* Marlow, the narrator of the story, makes a remark in passing, which I have always cherished as of profound significance. "It is when we try to grapple with another man's intimate needs that we perceive how incomprehensible, wavering and misty are the beings that share with us the sight of the stars and the warmth of the sun."

I suppose it is because I share that sentiment that I have always felt that academic training alone can never make an acceptable worker in the field of adult education. Unless, in addition to his formal education, he has an enormous liking for and understanding of all sorts and conditions of men he had better find his vocation elsewhere.

This may explain the fact that a great many of the men who have worked with us to make the CAAE the useful institution it has become were "Stickit ministers and Catholic priests." In Scotland, the "Stickit minister" was a man who had started his academic training with the idea of becoming a minister of the Presbyterian church and for any one of a number of reasons had become a "dominie," a school teacher, instead.

In fact, someone has said that in the early days of Scotland's history it was the "Stickit minister" who gave the Scottish educational system the high standards it has always maintained.

In my own case I had given up all hope of continuing as a minister of the Presbyterian Church a few months after my ordination. There were several reasons for this. To begin with I had taken my theological training at the Presbyterian College in Montreal at a time when the teaching staff of that institution was made up of men, some of whom were among the greatest scholars in their fields of that time. Professors D. J. Fraser, in New Testament, MacIntosh in Old Testament, Welch in comparative religions, and Johnston Ross, in Church History and Philosophy of Religion, were men of profound learning. They were fearless and outspoken critics of many of the accepted and cherished doctrines of the Church. They tore the Westminster Confession of Faith with its pagan concepts of "calling and election," "fore-ordination," "pre-destination," etc., into tatters, to the immense satisfaction of all of us.

During my undergraduate days also there had been a notorious heresy trial in Montreal, as a result of which one of the ablest professors in the Methodist Theological College, Dr. G. C. Workman, had been compelled to resign his chair because he had openly questioned the validity of some of the fundamental doctrines of the Methodist church. Shortly after the trial I heard Dr. H. M. Tory, in an address before a large group of students, condemn the action taken by the heresy hunters when he declared: "This is the sort of thing that forces many honest seekers after truth to be anti-ecclesiastic in order *not* to be anti-Christian."

All this was very unsettling, but my main difficulty, I think, was that I had always believed that a minister of the gospel ought to have some, at least, of the attributes of Sainthood, and I was beginning to realize that I had none. One of my senior colleagues in the Theological College with whom I discussed my problem analyzed it quite simply; he said, "My boy you have never been converted." And I am inclined to think he was right.

I came back from World War I convinced that I was not fitted either in temperament or in conviction to continue as a minister of the Presbyterian Church. But I also knew that I wanted above all to work with people. After all, I had descended from a long line of parsons, and the urge to help make the world a better place to live in was bred in my bones. The job offered me at the University of Alberta in 1920 seemed to be the kind of opportunity I was looking for.

I suppose the desire to see people and situations change and grow is the motive which leads most men and women into education, welfare work, the church, and other altruistic endeavours. It is certainly not the love of money. In adult education I have found an outlet for whatever gifts of heart and mind God and my ancestors gave me. If I have a working philosophy of adult education it is based on the conviction that the desire for knowledge is a normal human appetite, and that the capacity to acquire knowledge continues throughout life. I also know from long experience that through study, discussion and planning together people can change their social and economic environment and in so doing change themselves.

Hundreds of articles have been written defining the goals of adult education. Many of them are clothed in such incomprehensible jargon that the average individual, if he bothers to read them at all, understands little of what they have to say. Actually the objectives of adult education like any other set of ideas having to do with human behaviour can be expressed in the simplest language.

Some years ago, Dr. M. M. Coady of St. Francis Xavier University and I collaborated in producing, what seemed to us at the time, a fairly adequate statement of the objectives of adult education. I write these down here for what they are worth.

(a) That the individual, his rights, his moral and spiritual significance, is of supreme importance in a democracy.

(b) That social progress can only come about through improvement in the quality of human beings, and that improvement can only come through education.

(c) That adult education must suit its efforts to the intimate interests of the individual or the group, and in most instances these interests are economic.

(d) That adult education functions most effectively through group study and group action.

(e) That the ultimate objective of all education, particularly adult education, is the development of the individual's capacity to live a fuller and more abundant life.

(f) That education, like religion, can only be truly vital in the measure of its freedom from external authority.

After my retirement in 1951, my former associate, Dr. J. R. Kidd, became Director. Under his able and dedicated direction the Canadian Association for Adult Education has expanded enormously and has more than fulfilled the dream of its founders.

Many of the leaders in the movement whose names have appeared in these pages have disappeared from the scene, their places taken by younger men. Methods have changed to suit the demands of a new age, but the quality of leadership is of the same high standard and the organization occupies a proud position not only in Canada but abroad.

In E. M. Forster's book, *Two Cheers for Democracy,* there is an essay called "What I believe," and in it the author makes this statement. I take the liberty of quoting it here as an expression of my own belief.

I believe in aristocracy—not an aristocracy of power, based upon rank and influence, but an aristocracy of the sensitive, the considerate and the plucky. Its members are found in all nations and classes and through all ages, and there is a secret understanding between them when they meet. They represent the true human tradition, the one permanent victory of our queer race over cruelty and chaos."